MW00328690

THE DIVINE REVERSAL

RECOVERING THE VISION OF JESUS CHRIST AS THE LAST ADAM

CALEB MILLER

Father's House Press
ISBN: 978-0-9916265-0-2

TABLE OF CONTENTS

Cover Design by: Lori Evans

The Divine Reversal ©2014
Caleb Miller

Editing by: Thom Cooper, Carolyn Kistner, Mary Munoz & Mike Miller

Published by Father's House Press
2649 E Mulberry 18/19
Fort Collins, CO 80524

Printed and bound in the United States of America

"The question is not so much how "Adam's" sin affects us, as how Christ's forgiveness (which we are charged to make real) affects Adam"

James Alison
The Joy of Being Wrong: Original Sin through Easter Eyes

FOREWORD

SUGGESTING TO EVANGELICAL CHRISTIANITY the need to rethink doctrines that have compromised, for the world, the efficacy of Christ's redemption is risky business. To witness your own son presenting the challenge can be as emotionally stressful as hearing he has taken to bungee jumping into canyons, skydiving or back country extreme skiing. You realize the potential dangers (in this case, rejection, exclusion from mainline consideration, and labels applied by the doctrinal police bullies). The difference here however is that this is not simply the whim of a thrill seeking, adrenaline junky. This is the necessary response of a thinking generation that has taken seriously the failure of the Church to embrace the whole of humanity with the embrace of Christ.

Marilyn and I have used our freedom to think and speak outside the box for four decades and we have encouraged Caleb not to be contained even within the enlarged arena of our understanding. We are thankful that he has heeded our advice because we realize that the "elders" do not have all knowledge and understanding and we too have much to learn. The Father waits with excitement for questioning hearts to *"ask of Him that He might give them the nations as their inheritance"*. These pages reveal the sincerity of Caleb's personal inquiry of The Father and give much needed direction to the reformation of thought that will reframe our Gospel to the world so that the world might once again hear the Gospel from Christ's perspective. Needless to say we are proud of our son but also of the other youthful voices now engaging "exclusive" religious dialogue with a sense of The Father's heart for all of mankind. Read this book and be as blessed as we were when we heard these messages delivered first as Caleb preached to the congregation of Father's House Ministries.

Mike and Marilyn Miller
Word of Grace Ministries

PRAISE FOR THE DIVINE REVERSAL

For all of us, life is a journey through which we continue to move, grow, mature, change, and become transformed. The most important, transforming, and life-changing part of our journey takes place upon the road we travel with God – a road that He has determined will never end. For far too many, however, a point is often reached where a person believes he has gone as far as he wants, or perhaps even needs, to go and instead of continuing to journey with the Lord, he decides to set up camp and travel no farther. How sad and tragic it is for the individual who has determined to remain in his camp, for he will never know what glorious beauty he might have seen just around the next bend if he had chosen to continue his journey with Jesus. If you find that you might be one of those individuals who has set up camp and has not moved beyond that point in a very long time, then Caleb's book will challenge you to pull up stakes, rejoin Jesus on your journey, and see what stunning view awaits you just around the next bend.

- Thomas M. Cooper, co-founder of Anchor Ministries and author of *What is the Meaning of This?!*

In that part of Christianity known as the 'grace movement' many have found freedom from moral legalism but are still in bondage to theological legalism. With his own unique style, Caleb Miller tackles the problem head on demonstrating that the proclamation of the gospel begins with God, not ourselves, and in so doing emphasizes the great salvation for the entire human race wrought in Jesus Christ. If you are interested in just how great God's salvation is, then you will want to read this book.

- Michael Hardin, Executive Director, Preaching Peace and author of *The Jesus Driven Life* and *What the Facebook?*

There are many echoes in modern Christendom; voices that rephrase important things others have said. There's nothing wrong with that at all. Some things need to be said again and again in order to impact the pervasive legalism of our culture. Different voices repeating the same message is important. On the other hand, there are leading voices that set the pace in the growing grace revolution sweeping our world right now.

With the publication of The Divine Reversal, an important leading voice is emerging. I predict that this first book by Caleb Miller will be widely received by many with an appetite for a more robust understanding of the greatness of Divine Agape. With a passion for clarity and an intellectual acumen for depth, Caleb leads us into the very heart of the gospel.

What is this divine reversal discussed in this book? It is the finished work of Jesus Christ that undoes the havoc caused by Adam. It is the celebration of the adoption of humanity and our restoration to innocence in the person of the Last Adam. It is the good news that causes the hearts of believers to jump for joy; the announcement to seekers that they have already been found; the *divine notice to antagonists that their rejection isn't as big as their Father's acceptance. It is the gospel.*

Open your heart to the message of this book and you will be transformed, for this is a book that presents the Light that has come into this world enlightening every person. That Light will become a Midday Sun for many who have stood in the shadows of religion as they read these chapters.

- Dr. Steve McVey, Grace Walk Ministries

CALEB MILLER

A NOTE FROM THE AUTHOR

ANY AUTHORS FROM MANY different religious upbringings, theological standpoints and diverse doctrinal backgrounds are coming out in force with books about heaven, hell, eternal salvation or the error of this-or-that doctrine.

This book is not meant to be yet another in the pile of literature that is rapidly gathering on desks of ministers across the religious plane (including my own). Many of these books are profound statements of doctrine, redefining the way we approach Christianity, Christ, and even how we look at God. Many are simply amazing statements of the successful work of Jesus, deep theological books about the nature and personhood of the Father, and writings that force us to delve into the deepest parts of our religious background and answer real questions about heaven, hell and the fate of humanity. This book, however, is not meant to be one of those books.

Instead, this book is intended to accomplish but one thing, that is, to help us begin to reset some of our *system defaults* so that we can begin to approach our faith, our religious activity, and even our societal undertakings with a fresh, gospel-laden methodology, looking at things through the lens of the very One that Paul referred to as "the last Adam".

I am someone who has taken off a portion of my religious lens (none of us can claim that we have taken all of them off) and begun to look at the bible, the Savior, the Father, and life with a new set of lenses. These lenses may still be tarnished by my humanity; but nonetheless, they are a new set of lenses.

From time to time I will venture to use Greek and Hebrew words. I am no ancient language scholar, and I fully understand that sometimes the meaning of a word remains hidden, lost in time due to cultural misunderstanding and societal context we simply cannot view. When this is the case, we must simply use the tools available, and be willing to bend our own understanding when the circumstance arises. Context often dictates a more appropriate meaning than the bare meaning itself. What do I mean by that? Take the word *love* for example. In our current vernacular, love can mean extreme like, deep affection, or if spoken sarcastically, hate. The meaning is dictated by the context surrounding it.

I will often employ the use of scripture attributed to the Apostle Paul. I fully understand that much of this scripture is of questionable Pauline origin, but I still choose to use his name when referring to the author. Why do I do this? Biblical Historicity is important, but the point I am trying to make in this book is not historical authorship accuracy, but rather the efficacy of Jesus Christ and His work on behalf of mankind.

But enough about me, we should talk about these system defaults and how we can reset them a bit in our gospel approach.

CALEB MILLER

THE PENDULUM

"For the longest way round is the shortest way home."
C.S. Lewis (Mere Christianity).

THERE IS A PHENOMENON that takes place among the body of Christ that I call *The Great Pendulum*. It goes a little something like this:

1.   A man (who is usually after something more from God, to better his own existence, or to better the lives of those around him) receives a revelation from God. That point of revelation is the resting spot of the pendulum.

2.   The people who follow the man begin to make the revelation (of rest) something that they must do to achieve (e.g. - you *must* give to receive - so they start giving only to receive).

3.   The people who do not follow the man see the abuse that his followers have begun to unleash on humanity. They take the pendulum and swing it as fast and hard as possible to the opposite extreme.

This scenario is all too common. It happens to those *grace* folks, as well as the *legalists*. None can escape its forceful swing. What starts as a revelation from God, delivered to a man during a time of rest, is bent, twisted and perverted into a rewards-based work. There are literally too many of these types of doctrines to list. Just rest assured that any area that a particular minister seems to have a (larger than what would be considered normal) hang-up in is an area where this pendulum shifts and begins its downswing.

We can think of it like this: There is a ride at a particular amusement park in the State of Texas that is a giant pirate ship. The ride begins with about 50 people on each side, facing each other. As it begins its swing, you can feel the tension in the ship and among the people aboard. The tension rises as the ship rises and releases as the ship comes to the middle point again. And it is only when the ride is over that you are really back at a place of rest.

I believe God is saying that it is time for the ride to end, that it is time for us all to get off the ship, push reset, and stop making wild rides out of what we think we heard.

RESET

Computer manufacturers put system defaults in place. They accomplish one goal ... to make the system run at optimum speed and performance, as well as ease for the broadest audience. There are certain system defaults that can be changed without causing harm to the system while others will shut the whole thing down, and render it useless until those defaults are reset.

Because we simply trust that the manufacturer knew what they were doing when they built the machine, we probably never dig deep enough into our computer manual to discover the system defaults. Most of us will leave those system defaults in place, never adjusting what the manufacturer put in place. (If you are like me however, you probably tinker to the point of near annihilation of your system, and have to do forced resets from time to time!)

If only it were this simple in the Christian life, that we could push a big red button to reset our defaults to the guaranteed approved settings. However, we cannot. We are living some 2000 years after Jesus came to earth as incarnate grace. We are living thousands of years after the writing of scripture. Many system defaults have been played with in those thousands of years; some by prying children's hands, who had no right digging around in our system defaults; and some by people who desired to change things for their own benefit, *spiritual hackers* if you will. We need to undo much of what has been done, and bring ourselves back to a point of understanding the simple truth of the gospel of grace, its unconditional nature, and reality of the power of the sacrifice of the Son.

Allow yourself to reset your defaults. Let the Holy Spirit guide you into all the truth, direct you to the heart of the matter, and in all wisdom – test all things. When resetting centuries old default settings, we cannot expect this journey to be quick; it takes time. We cannot change the dogmatic ship we are all on with a few words, books, songs, or teachings. But, we will never change it without them. We must keep moving forward, keep fighting, and never stop growing. A teacher does himself no good when he ceases to learn for himself because he must keep teaching.

On with the show!

CHAPTER 1
LOST?

I have gone astray like a lost sheep; Seek Your servant, for I do not forget Your commandments. - **Psalm 119:176**

OR CENTURIES, THE Christian church has traveled the world, built massive empires, amassed land, money, and possessions, all in an effort to do one simple thing - to win *the lost*. But, what if there is something about all this that we are ignoring? What if we are simply re-doing something that has already been done?

This creates a bit of a conundrum for the typical Christian mindset. We have spent our lives trying to do this...the very same thing Jesus did.

In order to reset ourselves a little bit, we should look into what the bible has to say about the lost; and more importantly, what it does not have to say.

In the Old Testament, there are 3 words used for *lost*:
- abedah - *a lost thing*
- naphal - *to fall*
- abad - *to perish, vanish, go astray, or be destroyed (as in a lost and wandering sheep).*

Jeremiah 50:6 - *My people have been lost sheep. Their shepherds have led them astray; they have turned them away [on] the mountains. They have gone from mountain to hill; they have forgotten their resting place.*

We are given a view in Jeremiah of what the Father views as lost, that is, those who have been led astray by the shepherds and have forgotten where it is they could find rest. This is the very place David spoke of in Psalm 23, the green pastures that the only shepherd we are supposed to follow takes us toward. Many "believers" of our day would fall under this type of *lost*; many who claim to know Christ, would still appear as *lost* in this realm. Too many have forgotten their place of rest, the place where no more works are demanded, where nothing is expected of us except to bask in the love of the eternal Father.

Ezekiel 34:16 - *"I will seek what was lost and bring back what was driven away, bind up the broken and strengthen what was sick; but I will destroy the fat and the strong, and feed them in judgment."*

Here Ezekiel gives us a word of prophecy about what the Father is heading toward in the person of Jesus Christ; that He *will seek what was lost and bring back what was driven away.* The important point about this is coming in the next few verses. *(As a side note, the fat and the strong are not people, they are attitudes of greed and self-reliance, but we are not speaking of that yet!)*

Psalm 119:176 - *I have gone astray like a lost sheep; Seek Your servant, for I do not forget Your commandments.*

It seems as though David understood what the Father was up to. He did not ask the Father to draw him back; he did not ask the Father to give him the magic potion to please Him. He did not even say *through my belief or faith;* he simply said, *seek your servant.*

The word *seek* means: *to take pains for preserving the life of another.* Do we get that? This is what the Father is about. This is what He was leading towards in the gospel in the person of Jesus Christ. He is leading us to a point of where HE is going to take great pains in order to preserve OUR lives for us.

Throughout the Old Testament, we are left with a very small picture of what western Christianity would refer to as *the lost*. There are several references to lost items being restored among the books of the law, several references to women who have either lost their children, or lost their ability to bear children, but in reference to lost people, this is it. A total of 4 references are found concerning people: 2 in Ezekiel, 1 in Jeremiah, and 1 in Psalms. For our purposes the picture we are to grasp is the one of Jeremiah - that there are lost sheep among the house of Israel; and the one of Ezekiel - that the Father is going to seek out that which is lost; and finally the picture of David - that the Father is going to take pains to preserve the life of the lost. Let us now quickly jump to the New Testament idea of *lost*.

In the New Testament there are also 3 words used for *lost*:

- moraino - *to be foolish, to make flat and tasteless. (As in salt losing its flavor)*
- apollymi - *to destroy, to put out of the way entirely, abolish, put an end to, ruin, render useless, to kill etc.*
- ginomai - *to become, to come into existence (again with salt losing its saltiness as the reference – to become salt-less).*

(There are two verses where Jesus is referring to salt losing its flavor, once using *moraino*, the other using *ginomai*. Every other occurrence of lost in the New Testament is the word *apollymi*.)

Matthew 10:5-6 - *These twelve Jesus sent out and commanded them, saying: "Do not go into the way of the Gentiles, and do not enter a city of the Samaritans. "But go rather to the lost sheep of the house of Israel."*

Here Jesus is speaking to His disciples, giving them instruction as to what they are called to do. They are sent forth to begin what Ezekiel prophesied the Father was going to do through Christ, to gather up the *lost sheep* of the house of Israel - those of whom Jeremiah spoke - who had been driven out by their shepherds, or religious leaders; those who had forgotten (or *lost*) their place of rest.

Matthew 15:24 - *But He answered and said, "I was not sent except to the lost sheep of the house of Israel."*

Christ is setting forth that for which He was sent - *the lost sheep of the house of Israel*. Is Jesus saying He is not the savior of the world? No! He is simply making a statement of what His ministry on this earth is all about. This is incredibly important to remember as we study Jesus' teachings, His actions, and even His prayers. He is ministering to, for, and about the house of Israel. He is not speaking things that you and I can understand today; we are not a part of that house; and we are not those lost sheep. All too often we can fall into the trap of trying to frame our own salvation through the lens of first century Judaism. Without being a scholar in that field, we really ought to leave it alone. But I digress, moving on...

> Matthew 18:11-12 - *For the Son of Man has come to save that which was lost. "What do you think? If a man has a hundred sheep, and one of them goes astray, does he not leave the ninety-nine and go to the mountains to seek the one that is straying?*

Again, Christ is telling us what He is here to do: to *save that which was lost.* What we need to grasp here is something of paramount importance. First, Jesus does not say He came to save *those who were lost*; He says *that which was lost. Those* carries with it the mindset of a set group of people, while *that* carries the idea it is a single thing He came to save. Second, Jesus does not say He came to give that which was lost an avenue of getting saved, or a method of salvation. He says He came to save that which was lost; or in other words, it is His job to save. This is so important. If Jesus had only come so we might have an avenue of getting saved, then it is still up to us to find the avenue, walk it, and come to the end result. However, He came to save. When He spoke *it is finished* on the cross, He literally meant that everything He had been sent to do was accomplished, His saving, His fulfillment of the law and prophets, His work on earth - all finished, needing nothing more added to it. The peace which He said He gave, not as the world gives, was once and for all delivered to mankind, regardless of the fact we murdered Him unjustly!

> **John 17:12** - *While I was with them in the world, I kept them in Your name. Those whom You gave Me I have kept; and none of them is lost except the son of perdition, that the Scripture might be fulfilled.*

(There is a little confusion surrounding this verse, and unless we read the next chapter of John, it really makes very little sense.)

> **John 18:9** - *that the saying might be fulfilled which He spoke, "Of those whom You gave Me I have lost none."*

In John 17:2 Jesus is praying to the Father, knowing the time has come for Him to fulfill all things. He made the statement *those whom you gave me;* and the religious world has a heyday with it, leaving out the context of John's writing. In chapter 18, Judas has betrayed Jesus and led the Roman guard to Him in the garden. Peter then draws his sword, cutting off the ear of the one guard and Jesus steps in telling Peter to lower his sword to prevent any further violence from taking place. This is when we see *of those whom you gave me I have lost none.* What Jesus is simply saying here is this: these disciples You (Father) have led to follow me have not met their physical death through my life. Jesus is foreshadowing something that Paul would say later on that if one died for all, then all died. He knew they could not die on His account, because soon enough, they would all be in Him on the cross, dying with Him at the same time. Because their death was to be consummated in His, He was making the statement that their death could not happen on His account.

What about this *son of perdition* though? This is Judas. He is the one to whom Jesus refers when He says *none is lost except the son of perdition.* Jesus is not saying Judas is beyond salvation; He is saying Judas life will end before His own. Judas is a peculiar part of the gospel. His name literally means *he will be praised.* In Hebrew, praised means to shine. Judas' name literally means *He will shine!* Whether or not Judas was *predestined* to betray Christ is not something I believe we need to discuss. However, just the meaning of His name says so much. Through this one man, Jesus was turned over. Through His turning over, He became the shining light that pierced through our darkness once and for all! Moving to Luke we see even more.

Luke 19:10 - *For the Son of man is come to seek and to save that which was lost.*

Again, there are two things of which we need to take note here

- First, remember what David asked of the Lord in Psalm 119? That the Father would seek him? What did the word *seek* mean? *To take pains for preserving anyone's life.* We always need to remember Jesus was ministering to, in, and for the house of Israel. As a Jew, and one who studied in the temple, Jesus would have had much, if not all, of the Old Testament memorized. Nothing He said was an accident. When He said *to seek that which was lost,* He is making a statement, knowing full well the Jewish mind would immediately make the parallel to the Psalms, and knew what *seek* meant to a Hebrew person. We should do the same, because we will find out something beautiful. Jesus is saying He has come to take pain for preserving the life and to save that which was lost.

- Second, once again Jesus is not saying He has come to give the lost an avenue of salvation. He is not saying that He is giving them a part of the equation of *getting saved.* He makes a purposeful statement that He has come to save, period, with nothing else added. This is tough for religion because we so desperately desire to add something to our saved position, but we just cannot. When we make something the door by which we access *getting saved,* we have just made that thing a work, and a mockery of the sacrifice of Christ.

This works even in the realm of belief. Belief does not change what is true about you; it simply places you in line with what is already true. You do not go from *unsaved* to *saved* (in the typical way that we have presented it); you go from an *unbeliever* to a *believer* about what is already true about you. Your belief does not make Jesus the Son of God. Your belief does not crucify Him for all mankind. Your belief does not raise Him from the dead. He did all those things; and your belief acknowledges those truths, confirming them in your own heart and mind. Faith, which we will get into deeper later in this book, simply lays hold of what the Father has already provided through His grace.

2 Corinthians 4:3 - *But even if our gospel is veiled, it is veiled to those who are perishing.*

This is the final time (as well as the only time outside the gospels) the word *lost* is used in the remainder of the New Testament. We would expect, with all the emphasis the church has placed on "winning the lost", that there would be page after page filled with references to those lost souls we are to be winning. Certainly there must be some command somewhere in there? Maybe we should quickly look at this together.

2 Corinthians 4 is a chapter in which Paul is outlining their ministry together, his and the people at Corinth, when he makes this statement. Paul simply says *if* our gospel is veiled it is only veiled to those who are perishing. Simply, veiled means hidden or misunderstood. Paul is saying if the

gospel is misunderstood, it is misunderstood by those who are perishing. Next comes *if.* What a large word for just two letters. This is not a definitive statement; it is saying the gospel should not be veiled. But if it is, it is only because those hearing it are perishing. Why are they perishing? Well, the next verse quickly outlines why... *because they do not believe.* This says exactly what we just discussed about believers and unbelievers. When we believe we align ourselves with what is already true about us, unveiling the gospel to our hearts, minds and eyes. When we are unbelieving it is so because our minds have been blinded or veiled by the enemy. *Blinded minds* means blunted mental discernment.

Much of today's church would fall under this category. Their mental discernment has been blunted with so much being added to the cross; it has ceased to be the answer for all we face, and has become a starting point for work upon work upon work. We are rapidly and sadly approaching a time when we are becoming just like those lost sheep of the house of Israel. We have forgotten the place of rest that has been provided, and have begun adding to the cross - even with things like faith and belief.

Is belief necessary? Absolutely! However the gospel makes no demands of you except that it also supplies the answer. In hearing the word of grace and the truth of the cross, belief is supplied; and in hearing the power of Jesus Christ, faith comes forth from within. Therefore, faith and belief are fruits of knowing Him, never prerequisites to it. We can also say it this way; we can never make ourselves into something by faith that He has not already made us by His grace. Isaiah tells us *by His stripes you were (past tense) healed*, signifying that we can be healed because He has made us healed. More on this concept later!

So, we are not really left in a world of *saved* and *unsaved*, *lost* and *found*, or *in* and *out*. We are left in a world of believers and unbelievers. We are left with those to whom the gospel is veiled, and those to whom it is not. We do not need to throw away all our terminology; however, we do need to rethink our approach in how we deal with those we would call *lost*. If our gospel is misunderstood, those who are unbelievers misunderstand it. Only the light of the true gospel can bring them to a place of belief.

CHAPTER 2
WHAT MUST BE TRUE ABOUT YOU

"My son, you are always with me, and all that I have is yours"
Luke 15:31

W E HAVE LEARNED TWO things about what Christianity has called *the lost*.

1. That Jesus came for the lost sheep of the house of Israel, and He ministered to those people. All of His ministry on this earth must be viewed through that lens.

2. That, according to Paul, the fact the gospel is veiled to us, in any fashion, puts us under the

category of *the lost;* or as he put it, *those who are perishing.*

2 Corinthians 4:3 - *But even if our gospel is veiled, it is veiled to those who are perishing.*

Much of our *Christian* church today still falls under this category, as ones with *blunted mental discernment* about areas of the gospel in our lives. Any area we are not seeing the fullness of what Jesus Christ has provided is an area of darkness, an area in which the gospel is veiled. This is not condemnation; this is hope. The hope is that through one simple thing the darkness, or veiling of our minds, can be removed. And what is that thing? Belief.

Let us grasp something together shall we? The bible and the gospel are two different things. The gospel reveals your inclusion into the life, love and fellowship of the Trinity, apart from your works, while the bible (incorrectly used) tells you what *you must do* in order to be *in.* The gospel reveals the bible. And, it is quite possible to preach out of the bible without ever preaching the gospel, but it is nearly impossible to preach the gospel without the use of the bible in some manner. We must get this straight because Paul does not say if the *scripture* is veiled. He says *gospel.* What is the gospel? We have heard that it is the *almost too good to be true news.* But, the Greek word for gospel means *the proclamation of the grace of God manifest and pledged in Christ ...* God's grace, incarnated in the Son, pledged in His very existence and proclaimed by His work. If this is veiled, it is veiled to we who are perishing in some fashion.

I purposely passed over one passage that dealt with the *lost* in the New Testament. I saved it for now because there is so much packed into this one chapter of Luke that it warrants its own time with no other distraction. We should take the time to go through Luke 15. In this chapter, Jesus is speaking something beautiful and powerful in regards to *the lost* in this chapter that deserves our attention.

Before we go into this, we need to set some ground rules regarding parables. (These are bendable rules, and that is fine. I feel we are allowed to play with the word and make it suit our understanding, it certainly worked for Paul and Christ!)

- First, in every parable, there is a main character - e.g. *a certain man* or *there was a man* or *a sower.* Jesus uses this character to describe and relate the Father to people in a language they can understand.
- Second, the object of the parable - e.g. *a sheep* or *two sons* or *a coin,* as we will see in the coming verses, represents humanity, mankind, the creation of God.

Understanding this, we will now get into these verses.

Luke 15:1-3 - *Then all the tax collectors and the sinners drew near to Him to hear Him. And the Pharisees and scribes complained, saying, "This*

Man receives sinners and eats with them." So He spoke this parable to them, saying:

I am going to break in here and say a few things. Jesus had a unique effect on the people who were around Him. The religious were repulsed and the sinners were included. When we are told the sinners drew near to Him, it literally means that they were joined with Him. They were included in what He was speaking - those whom we would call *lost*. The Pharisees had an issue with His inclusion. Once again, they said something we do not get.

Receives sinners means more than just accepts them. Literally, it points to intercourse and companionship or acceptance with no chance of rejection. The *sinners* of the day knew He held something out to them that no man could ever take away. That message is what speaks to our hearts today, and calls from within us that we are included. The offense of Jesus eating with *the sinners* is a cultural offense we do not understand in western society. A Jew would only eat with those they were prepared to call family. Jesus is calling these *sinners* family!

> **V4-7** - *"What man of you, having a hundred sheep, if he loses one of them, does not leave the ninety-nine in the wilderness, and go after the one which is lost until he finds it? And when he has found it, he lays it on his shoulders, rejoicing. And when he comes home, he calls together his friends and neighbors, saying to them, 'Rejoice with me,*

for I have found my sheep which was lost!' I say to you that likewise there will be more joy in heaven over one sinner who repents than over ninety-nine just persons who need no repentance.

This first parable points directly back to what we discussed earlier ... Jesus was sent for whom? *For the lost sheep of the house of Israel.* He says it a few times, and then once again, reaffirms this statement with His first parable. He is not making some roundabout statement, trying to get them to understand something they do not know. He is purposely using sheep as a reference to the verses that the Pharisees and scribes had written down so often, and the very people who rewrote and memorized the Old Testament. He is letting them know *I am He of whom the prophets spoke. I am here to seek what was lost, to bind up what was broken.*

We miss something here that Jesus says right back in the face of the Pharisees. Just as they have said *He receives sinners*, He says back to them *rejoice with me*. Rejoice speaks of joining in, or drawing near. He is making an intentional and literal affront to their problem with the *sinners*. He is saying, just as they draw near to me, I invite others to join in my joy when they draw near. Jesus is all about inclusion. Something we fail to see today.

Jesus then assaults their religious legalism and self-righteousness with one word. *Just.* He is not saying there are 99 people who are good enough and have no need of repentance in their lives. The word *just* means something a little more damaging to the character of these Pharisees.

Literally – *Of those who seem to be righteous to themselves, who pride themselves as being righteous, who pride themselves in their virtues, whether real or imagined.* Jesus has just slapped the face of religion with this statement. He told this to those who pride themselves on their ability to uphold (or change as needed) the law. Almost sarcastically, He tells them that heaven rejoices more over one person who realizes they need Christ rather than the 99 who in all their self-righteousness and pride, think they can do it on their own, or have some part to play in it. Let's go on.

> **V8-10** *"Or what woman, having ten silver coins, if she loses one coin, does not light a lamp, sweep the house, and search carefully until she finds it? And when she has found it, she calls her friends and neighbors together, saying, 'Rejoice with me, for I have found the piece which I lost!' Likewise, I say to you, there is joy in the presence of the angels of God over one sinner who repents."*

I love what Jesus does here. He again assaults the religion of these men by three simple words. *Or what woman.* They may not have understood; but He did. He was intentionally saying something here. The author did not hear God wrong when writing the book of Genesis *in the image of God He created them, male and female.* The female image of God deserves looking into. We do not have the time now but we need to understand that over and over again, God says *I am not a man that I should....*God is genderless, not a sexual being like humanity. This approach has caused much uprising in Wm Paul Young's book *The Shack;* and, I for one am glad it has. This topic needs to be discussed, but not now – at least not in this book!

Now when Jesus says this woman *sweeps the house,* He is referring to the place of dwelling, as well as the inhabitants who dwell there. The Greek language speaks this way in several places. When Paul says Jesus *led captivity captive,* the word *captivity* says the same thing; the place of captivity as well as the one who holds people there. In the book of Revelation when John speaks of Jesus saying, *I am He who ... holds the keys of death and of Hades* – again, he is referring to the place of the dead, as well as the one who holds people there. This is an important concept to grasp, as the Father is not concerned with cleaning up the people so much as He is the place in which they live. He is concerned with them knowing where, and in whom, they have their home.

(There is something here of which we should take note. The literal text makes more of a reference to the statement that the woman makes saying, *Rejoice with me, I have found my lost piece.* This is important; and we will see why in just a bit.)

Now we will look together at what is one of my top three favorite stories in the bible. We know it as *the prodigal son.* There is so much to be said about this passage, and so many directions we could go. But we are speaking about *the lost,* so we will focus on that. We will come back here later and deal with the family identity; but for now, we will stay on the topic of those who are lost.

V11-16 *Then He said: "A certain man had two sons. And the younger of them said to his father, 'Father, give me the portion of goods that falls to me.' So he divided to them his livelihood. And not many days after, the younger son gathered all together, journeyed to a far country, and there wasted his possessions with prodigal living. But when he had spent all, there arose a severe famine in that land, and he began to be in want. Then he went and joined himself to a citizen of that country, and he sent him into his fields to feed swine. And he would gladly have filled his stomach with the pods that the swine ate, and no one gave him anything.*

The first thing to note in this story is this: *a certain man had two sons.* The Father has two sons … the nation of Israel and the Gentiles. We can also look at it this way: the legalists and us grace people - or the *in* and the *out.* Yet, in all of our titles, religious affiliations (or lack thereof) and confessions of faith, there is a truth lying right in front of us; *A certain man had two SONS.* Not one son and a servant, one son and a slave, one son and some other dude who lived in the home, but two sons. (We are never to disregard Israel as unimportant to the Father, any more than we would disregard our next-door neighbor as unimportant. The anti-Semitism in the church is disgusting and needs to be forever done away with.) We could stop here and get all we need but

I would like to see what Jesus is revealing about the Father and His position regarding *the lost*.

> **V17-19** *"But when he came to himself, he said, 'How many of my father's hired servants have bread enough and to spare, and I perish with hunger! I will arise and go to my father, and will say to him, "Father, I have sinned against heaven and before you, and I am no longer worthy to be called your son. Make me like one of your hired servants."'"*

As this son begins to realize what he has gotten himself into, he seems to remember what his pastor told him about repentance. If he wants his father to accept him again, he must come with all contrition, weeping and kneeling, ready to do penance for his sin. He begins making deals with the father in his head, just as many of us do from time to time when we find ourselves in sticky situations. *If you will heal (bless, take care of, insert special need here) me I will....* *(insert religious activity here). If you will save me, I will believe. If you will take me to heaven, I will confess Jesus Christ.* And like many of us, he seems quite content with the old adage, *Oh God, just let me serve you.*

> **V20-21** *"And he arose and came to his father. But when he was still a great way off, his father saw him and had compassion, and ran and fell on his neck and kissed him. And the son said to him,*

'Father, I have sinned against heaven and in your sight, and am no longer worthy to be called your son.'

Immediately, we have the picture of our Father that changes the game. This is Jesus, the guy who said *no one knows the Father but the Son,* giving us a clear picture of this Father He knows. His Father runs out while His son is far off; He does not wait for contrition, repentance or a statement of belief. He sees *(cherishes)* the son, runs *(to spend one's strength in performing or attaining something)* to him, meets him while he is still steeped in darkness, and has compassion. Literally, He is moved in His bowels with compassion, (that deep yearning we get when we see the starving kid on TV), falls on *(takes possession of)* His son, and kisses *(to join mouth to mouth)* him. It might seem odd to point out this is mouth to mouth but we must get what Jesus is saying. The Father so cherished the son that He spent His own strength to attain him. With deep compassion He takes possession of him, and before any act of repentance can come out, He kisses him. This sounds a lot like another passage of which we have forgotten the importance and power...*for God so loved the world...* (It is important to note: a dignified man of this era would not be seen running, showing exactly what the Father's heart is toward his son.)

The Father silences any confession, any placement of faith or blame, and all talk of servant-hood by kissing His son. He will not let a single word come out until He has expressed His undying love for the son. He is interested in one thing and one thing only - His son is home, and that he has once again joined the house as a part of the family (or we could say as one who is *included*).

> **V22-24** *"But the father said to his servants, 'Bring out the best robe and put it on him, and put a ring on his hand and sandals on his feet. And bring the fatted calf here and kill it, and let us eat and be merry; for this my son was dead and is alive again; he was lost and is found.' And they began to be merry.*

The son has just confessed his *sin* to the father. He has given a real act of repentance in our day and age. From our twisted view of the Father, we would expect Him to tell the boy ... as long as he has learned his lesson, or you are right, you have sinned. Yet the father does no such thing. He does not acknowledge the wrong done, not even so much as a word comes out of His mouth. Immediately, He changes the subject as if to say *I do not know what you are talking about*. He grants the boy a robe, a ring, and sandals. There are some things to note regarding what the Father has done here:

- The robe is a symbol of royalty or a position of power.
- The ring is a symbol of family and one who can act on behalf of the one whose signet it is.
- The sandals are only given to family members, not servants.

The father does not simply tell the son he is included; he gives him the proof without asking for a thing from him. He throws a party, not because the son has confessed his sin, but because he has come home. He throws a party because what was *lost* is now *found*.

V25-30 *Now his older son was in the field. And as he came and drew near to the house, he heard music and dancing. So he called one of the servants and asked what these things meant. And he said to him, 'Your brother has come, and because he has received him safe and sound, your father has killed the fatted calf.' "But he was angry and would not go in. Therefore his father came out and pleaded with him. So he answered and said to his father, 'Lo, these many years I have been serving you; I never transgressed your commandment at any time; and yet you never gave me a young goat, that I might make merry with my friends. But as soon as this son of yours came, who has devoured your livelihood with harlots, you killed the fatted calf for him.'*

Now for the first time, the older son comes on the scene. We need to note something about the first two parables here. Just as in the first parable about the sheep, there is one who is lost outside the home - the younger son, and in the parable of the coin, there is one who is lost inside the home - the older son. This older brother is so lost that he hears from a servant about the noise going on inside the home. He has not even bothered to come in; he is too busy doing his own thing. He is actually upset that his brother is home. He has not heard the circumstances surrounding his return, has not spoken to him and has not even gone to see him. But, he is mad nonetheless.

However, the father, being the father, does not demand that the older son come inside, but likewise he goes out to him. Just like he did with this younger son, the father goes to the older son, perfectly rounding out the picture of the father. He is far more interested in reaching out to us than demanding that we seek him, just as David saw the Father in Psalm 119 - *seek me Lord*. The brother has the audacity to call his own brother *this son of yours* trying to strip the boy of his identity in front of the father. He lies about him - *who has devoured your livelihood with harlots* (note the older brother was not with the younger, has not yet even talked with him about his escapades, and was not even in the same region as the younger brother); and instead of joining the festivities, he pouts.

> *V31-32 And he said to him, 'Son, you are always with me, and all that I have is yours. It was right that we should make merry and be glad, for your brother was dead and is alive again, and was lost and is found.'*

The father is always about restoring our identity, and not just ours, but also those who would fall under this category of the older brother who have viewed themselves as *in* and others as *out*. The father says *son*, and in one word tells the boy who he is to him. Then, he says *you are always with me and all that I have is yours*, as if to say, you have access to this party any time you want it. His final statement immediately restores the family bond, the identity of both sons, and seals what the story is all about ... *your brother was lost and is found*. The one who has just been told he is a son is told the other son is his brother, letting him know just as Jesus said in the beginning *a certain man had two SONS*. What is it we need to grasp in all this?

- A man had 100 sheep and one got lost - so he sought it out.
- A woman had 10 coins and one got lost - so she sought it out.
- A man had two sons and both were lost - so he sought them out.

You must understand that you can never be lost unless you already belong. It was the man's sheep, the woman's coin and the man's sons. They belonged to the characters. This is paramount. We have treated the ones we deemed as *lost* as though they do not belong until they say a sinner's prayer, and make some profession of belief. This should not be so. This is detrimental to the reality of the Father's heart. He seeks what is already His. He went through great personal pain to preserve the life of those who were lost *because* they already belonged, not to make them become something they were not already!

Also, it is quite possible to be *in* and still be *out* in some areas of our lives. We can be lost while inside the house. We can be lost while outside the house. The power of the gospel is this: we cannot be lost, except the Father will seek us out, find us, and restore us. His truth raises belief in our hearts, unveils the gospel to our minds, allows us to believe and opens the door to the truth. So either none are lost or, conversely, we are all lost from time to time. The good thing about this truth is found in Hebrews.

Hebrews 13:5b (AMP) - *for He God Himself has said, I will not in any way fail you nor give you up nor leave you without support. I will not, I will not, I will not in any degree leave you helpless nor forsake nor let you down relax My hold on you! Assuredly not!*

CALEBMILLER

CHAPTER 3

WHAT DETERMINES YOUR IDENTITY

"It is difficult to make a man miserable while he feels worthy of himself and claims kindred to the great God who made him."
Abraham Lincoln

WE MUST NOW LEARN to treat the word *lost* as a concept instead of a person. Lost is not a noun (a person, place or thing); it is an adjective (a means of describing a person, place or thing). It refers to something we can all fall under from time to time. Our identity is not determined by *lost* or *found*, *in* or *out*, *saved* or *unsaved*. Our identity is solely determined by one thing, our Father. We have no choice into which family we are born. No amount of confession, belief or faith caused us to be born. Our birth was determined by one thing, the thing with which we were predestined before there was time: *the adoption of children by Jesus Christ.* (Eph 1:5).

So then what do we need to do? We must redefine *lost.* Thinking about it naturally, there are two concepts we use: *Lost* and *Missing.* Missing is how we describe something or someone when *we* do not know where they are. Lost describes one who is somewhere they do not recognize, or what we would use when they do not know where they are standing.

None are missing to the Father; yet at any given time, all of us can be lost. We can all fall under this category of not comprehending our position. Paul said that the gospel can be veiled to us in some areas of our lives. This veiling happens for one reason, *we do not believe* (2 Cor 4:4). This means we must do but one thing to render ourselves *found...*just believe. But how can we, and what must we believe?

At this point in human history, as ridiculous as it may seem to me as I teach in a church, or even to one who reads this book, I must make the statement … we must believe in Jesus. At a minimum, you are reading because you believe there is something more. Of course we must believe, but this does not say anything to the world at large. It does not say what we must believe about Him, why or how, or answer any number of questions that arise about what He did. To me, saying something as simple as *believe in Jesus,* skirts the real issue, which is, where did He leave us? Did He come to earth as incarnate grace, do all He did, suffer death on a cross, mockery, betrayal, injustice, murder, and hell - just to leave us the way we were before He came? Just to leave us holding the keys of salvation ourselves? Just to leave us where we must now fulfill some new requirement of faith in order to be accepted by Him as His family? Or, did He come to earth to provide us with a new place of standing, with a new home, and a new identity? In other words, did He in fact come *to save that which was lost?*

WHAT WAS LOST?

Jeremiah 50:6 - *My people have been lost sheep. Their shepherds have led them astray; they have turned them away on the mountains. They have gone from mountain to hill; they have forgotten their resting place.*

What is lost to these people? Are they missing to the Father? Does He not know where they are? Or have they forgotten their position, or at this time, where they *could* stand? Nothing here is lost to the Father. They are not out of His line of sight, where He cannot find them. They are lost; they do not know where they stand and cannot see the place of rest. The place of rest is lost to them.

Luke 19:10 - *For the Son of man is come to seek and to save that which was lost.*

Jesus tells us just exactly what He is here to accomplish - to restore that which was lost. He guides us

45

back to that place of rest, the place in which we were always intended to remain. We can do one of two things to the people around us. We can either save them from hell *or* we can introduce them to the Father. The two are mutually exclusive. It is not our job to save people from hell; it was His. Our job is to introduce people to the Father and show them the place in which they stand. By introducing them to the means that delivers the end, we have taken care of the end and the means. But if we simply introduce them (through fear) to the end, we have missed the means altogether. They must know the place in which they stand. But where is that place?

THE HOUSE

I would like for us to build a house together, a place in which we can live, and, in order to be *found*, we must learn where it is we already live because of His grace.

> **Romans 4:24-5:2** - *but also for us. It shall be imputed to us who believe in Him who raised up Jesus our Lord from the dead, who was delivered up because of our offenses, and was raised because of our justification. Therefore, having been justified by faith, we have peace with God through our Lord Jesus Christ, through whom also we have access by faith into this grace in which we stand, and rejoice in hope of the glory of God.*

This place in which we stand is called *grace*. But we need to back up a bit, to discuss just how we got there because even in this passage, it would seem that our faith puts us into this grace.

Context is going to rear its head and we need to take note of it. In chronological sequence, it is understood that Paul wrote the book of Galatians before all his other letters, except the two to Thessalonica. Why is this important? Whether or not we realize or believe that Paul's letters were written to specific people groups about specific issues relating to their specific circumstances, the revelation Paul received and was preaching would have been understood by him as he moved forward. In the same fashion as us, when we receive a new revelation (to us) about the Father, that revelation then begins to define our other understanding. For example, when we began to see God as a God of love, as a God who *is* love, and as a Father who can only give love to us, this perception begins to redefine our existing insight into who He is and what He does. If we cannot process it through the lens of His love, it is not the Father. In this same light, we need to glance back at one of Paul's earliest writings, to the people of Galatia.

Galatians 2:20 (KJV) - *I am crucified with Christ: nevertheless I live; yet not I, but Christ liveth in me: and the life which I now live in the flesh I live by the faith of the Son of God, who loved me, and gave himself for me*

We purposely used the KJV here because it holds to the literal translation more clearly. It is the faith *of* the Son of God in which we live (*by* is literally *in*). Because of His great love, we now live in His faith. What does this mean for us?

Romans 12:3b - *God hath dealt to every man the measure of faith.*

We must now process Romans 4 through the lens of Galatians 2. Using Romans 12 as additional context, we can see what Paul is saying.

Romans 4:24-5:2 - *but also for us. It shall be imputed to us who believe in Him who raised up Jesus our Lord from the dead, who was delivered up because of our offenses, and was raised because of our justification. Therefore, having been justified by faith, we have peace with God through our Lord Jesus Christ, through whom also we have access by faith into this grace in which we stand, and rejoice in hope of the glory of God.*

Paul says in Romans 4 that Jesus was raised because of our justification. He goes on in chapter 5 to say that we have been justified by faith. Was it our faith then that raised Jesus from the dead? The way we preach faith and justification, and ignore the context of the scripture, it would appear so. No! It was the faith of Christ that raised Him, because our justification was completed. In the same manner, it is His faith through which we have peace with God, and access into this grace in which we stand. Still cannot believe it?

Ephesians 2:8 - *For by grace you have been saved through faith, and that not of yourselves; it is the gift of God*

We are saved by grace, the grace in which we stand, through faith. And this is the place the church stops reading. We do not care about context; we do not care about Paul's revelation. But he says it so plainly, so clearly that we must be ignoring the truth *intentionally* in this passage not to see it. *And that not of yourselves* - what is *that*? *Faith!* It is not our faith that saves us, or rather, saved us. It was the faith *of* Jesus Christ, which saved us, brought us into the family of God, rendered us all hopelessly and utterly *in*. If we are to say that we are saved by grace *and* faith, then we must absolutely understand that the *faith* we are referring to is Jesus' faith, and not our own. I am belaboring this point intentionally because we understand grace is not of us; and salvation is not of us. Somewhere along the line we have swallowed the story that faith is of us. It is just not. We need to grasp that there is nothing left for us to do to finish the already finished work!

Wall one of this new home in which we stand is called *grace*. Grace is this: the merciful kindness by which God, exerting his holy influence upon souls, turns them to Christ, keeps, strengthens and increases them in Christian faith, knowledge and affection, then, kindles them to the exercise of Christian virtues. Every way we slice this it is God doing the work, not us. Yet we still want to throw obligation on top of people to take them from *lost* to *found*.

> **Romans 3:21-22** - *But now the righteousness of God apart from the law is revealed, being witnessed by the Law and the Prophets, even the righteousness of God, through faith in Jesus Christ, to all and on all who believe. For there is no difference;*

Without even going into the literal text, we can see a problem within this verse. *To all, and on all who believe - for there is no difference.* No difference? Wait, we who believe love our private social club we have formed and called church. We love our status symbol of attending the largest church in the area. We love our titles and placement within the body. But there is no difference. If righteousness is only found through faith *in* Jesus, then how on earth can it be to all and on all who believe? But there is more. When we look at the literal text something is stated very clearly.

> **Romans 3:22 (KJV)** - *Even the righteousness of God, which is by faith of Jesus Christ unto all and upon all them that believe: for there is no difference.*

Once again, Paul is letting us know the context for faith. The faith *of* Jesus Christ renders us righteous. Neither our belief nor our faith puts us in this place we stand; rather, His faith puts us there once and for all.

Wall two of our new home is called *righteousness* - the state of him who is as he ought to be, righteous, the condition acceptable to God. And this condition, just as we have seen, is not provided by us, but was once and for all provided by Christ, through His faith and not our own, not of our works, not of our effort.

> **1 Thessalonians 3:12-13** - *And may the Lord make you increase and abound in love to one another and to all, just as we do to you, so that He may establish your hearts blameless in holiness before our God and Father at the coming of our Lord Jesus Christ with all His saints.*

We hold to a particular belief that something we do renders us holy, such as our observance of His commands, following the law, or walking in love. We have to intentionally be ignoring the truth in order to miss it; for once again, Paul lays it out so clearly for us. *That He may establish your hearts in holiness*...Not you, never you, but Him. And yet we still cling to our religion that something we do makes us holy. Somewhere we have made the association; our actions take us from *out* to *in*. Those who we might call *legalists* would say living a holy life makes you holy; or if you do not sin, then you are holy. We who claim to believe grace are just as bad. We slap a requirement of belief or faith on the position in which Christ has placed all mankind, as though their belief or faith is what took Him to the cross in the first place. Everything we believe about ourselves and where we find ourselves must be processed through the lens of the cross; it was not our choice that drove Him there, it was His love.

> **Colossians 1:21-22** - *And you, who once were alienated and enemies in your mind by wicked works, yet now He has reconciled in the body of His flesh through death, to present you holy, and blameless, and above reproach in His sight.*

He *has* reconciled. We have not been reconciled by our thoughts, confessions, beliefs, faith, hope, or any other activity. We were once and for all reconciled. And, His job is to present us as holy, blameless and above reproach. The Christian church has lived and preached as though this verse says Christ presents us holiness, blamelessness, and above reproachfulness (admittedly my own word). It is as though He shows us what is available to us if we will just fulfill our civic and religious duty here.

No, He presents us as:

- Holy - a most holy thing.
- Blameless - without blemish, faultless, "unblameable".
- Above reproach - that cannot be called into to account, unreproveable, unaccused, and blameless.

Most holy? Yes! He presents us just as holy as He is, as most holy! Unblameable? Yes! He presents us as ones who cannot be blamed for ANYTHING! Unreproveable? Yes! He presents us as those who cannot be corrected or reproved! In all of our negative thinking, we want to take these things as though all Jesus is presenting us as is without fault. This is true, but it is only half of the equation. He does present us without fault; but He also presents us as those who cannot be called into account for our good side as well. If our goodness, belief, or faith could render us *in* then our badness, unbelief and lack of faith can render us *out*. The same is true in reverse. We have given people a message that says we cannot possibly be good enough on our own; so Jesus was good for us. But unbelief and lack of faith will still take you out. We need to understand that if unbelief and a lack of faith can take us out, then our good actions could put us in. This cannot be so! It is Christ who presents us as utterly unblameable, for our good deeds or our bad, for our belief and faith, or lack thereof. His faith, His belief and His works brought us in, never ours.

Wall three of our new home is *holiness*, which is sanctification of heart and life. Jesus Christ has forever sanctified all of humanity through His saving faith ... not through our belief, not through our unbelief, but through His unwavering love and undying commitment to the reconciliation of humanity.

Ephesians 1:4 - *just as He chose us in Him before the foundation of the world, that we should be holy and without blame before Him in love.*

There are two phrases we will address; but for the purposes of building the fourth wall of our new home, we will look at *in love.* Paul says the Father chose us in Him (Christ) before the foundation of the world, before we could ever believe, have faith, or even breathe. Before our hearts struck their first beat, before we could think about Christ and what He did, before we could muster up faith or belief, the Father chose us in Him, to place us in love.

In - used of that which a person is surrounded, equipped, furnished, assisted, or acts. *Love.* We are placed in Love.

1 John 4:16 - *And we have known and believed the love that God has for us. God is love, and he who abides in love abides in God, and God in him.*

We are placed in Love, and thereby in Him. If God is love, then we are in Him. We must always remember this fact, because through love, all life and all we are flows. Paul tells us we are in Him in love; and John perfectly sums up by saying if we are in love, we are in Him. We cannot escape this fact. Wall four of our new home is love; and love is what opens the door to our hearts through Him.

Wall four of our new home is *love.* The affection, good will, love and benevolence of our Father is the door wall, the one with the opening in it. We do not enter through righteousness, holiness or even grace; we enter through love. Why? - Because God (and thereby Christ) is love. Our door is the Lord Jesus Christ through whom all may enter. When Jesus said *no man comes to the Father but by me,* He was telling us a message of hope. If no one can come except by Him, then all can come by Him.

What word sums this house up? *Reconciliation.* One thought must utterly encompass the truth of what the Father has provided through the Son, by His Spirit.

> **2 Corinthians 5:14-21** - *For the love of Christ compels us, because we judge thus: that if One died for all, then all died; and He died for all, that those who live should live no longer for themselves, but for Him who died for them and rose again. Therefore, from now on, we regard no one according to the flesh. Even though we have known Christ according to the flesh, yet now we know Him thus no longer. Therefore, if anyone is in Christ, he is a new creation; old things have passed away; behold, all things have become new. Now all things are of God, who has reconciled us to Himself through Jesus Christ, and has given us the ministry of reconciliation, that is, that God was in Christ reconciling the world to Himself, not imputing their trespasses to them, and has committed to us the word of reconciliation. Now then, we are ambassadors for Christ, as though God were pleading through us: we implore you on*

Christ's behalf, be reconciled to God. For He made Him who knew no sin to be sin for us, that we might become the righteousness of God in Him.

This passage so perfectly sums up our home and, if we present it to them correctly, the home of the whole world. If one died for all, then all died. Did one die for all? Yes. So all died. In that same fashion, He rose. So, all have risen. This means there is no more *old man* with which to struggle, no more *putting off Adam*, no more *crucifying your flesh*. All died, all rose in Him. Throughout this passage, the word *for* carries a literal definition of *on behalf of.* This changes things a bit. Because Christianity has for centuries told people that once they *get saved,* they must start living for God (as though God needed anything). But the truth is this: He died on our behalf; so we might live for Him, and no longer for ourselves.

This is why Paul can say, *we regard no man according to the flesh.* But what is it that we do every day in the judgment of those we have called lost? We judge their flesh by what they have said in the flesh, or where they go in the flesh, or what they do in the flesh. This is directly opposed to the gospel. We ought not to be judging anyone according to his or her flesh, but according to Him who died on behalf of all.

If anyone is in Christ he is a new creation. This is the lifeblood of those who cannot believe Jesus put all people in Him. However, Paul has just made the statement that *if one died for all, then all died,* and then follows it with *therefore.* This is a statement of conclusion not a statement of requirement! In conclusion, since all people are in Christ, they are a new creation, old things have passed away.... The gospel is not found in "ifs" but rather in "since". It is not "if" you do something, it is "since" He did everything! Now, look to the changing of subject. This passage begins and ends with people. Why then would we change the subject in the middle of a thought to *things?* We should not. Religion makes us fear what is being said here about people. Behold all *people* have become new and all *people* are of God, who has reconciled us. Paul says *us* in referring to human beings, not things. We must grasp this; it is of utmost importance if we are to begin to reveal to our fellow people (and even ourselves) our position in Christ, and take us from *lost* to *found.*

Paul then goes on to say something that still trips up the religious. He says: *God, who has reconciled us to Himself through Jesus Christ, and has given us the ministry of reconciliation, that is, that God was in Christ reconciling the world to Himself, not imputing their trespasses to them, and has committed to us the word of reconciliation.* The ministry of reconciliation is being tossed around as though it is some sort of heretical doctrine. However, it is the only thing we are given to do. We are here to preach the word of reconciliation to all mankind with this: *that God was in Christ reconciling the world to Himself, not imputing their trespasses to them.* Yet we still want to preach *for all have sinned and fallen short of the glory of God* to the world at large. God has committed to us who have at least seen His light the ministry of reconciliation. That reconciliation is this: Jesus, who was perfect, became our imperfection so we might be made perfect.

This *home* is where we all stand. It is a home of reconciliation - the restoration of the favor of God. That favor is poured out on this world, on those religion would label as the *in* and the *out,* the *lost* and the *found,* the *saved* and the *unsaved* and we are here to proclaim it; His reconciliation is for all. There is no separation with God. There is only union. As we have been made to be in union with the Godhead, we have also been made in union with one another, removing "the wall of separation" as Paul puts it.

CHAPTER 4

ALL INCLUSIVE GRACE

"For God so loved the WORLD…"
John 3:16

NOW THAT WE HAVE a proper starting point, we can begin our discussion of our Father and His grace. We have a great big God. He is so big, so loving and His love encompasses all of us. ALL of us. We have made some pretty big strides in revealing the depths of His love and grace. We say things like 'for God so loved THE WORLD' and all, amen. We know God's love includes everyone. We know that nothing can separate us from His love. We know that *neither death, nor life, nor angels, nor principalities, nor powers, nor things present, nor things to come, nor height, nor depth, nor any other creature, shall be able to separate us from the love of God, which is in Christ Jesus our Lord.* – (**Rom 8:38-39**)

But what about grace?
How inclusive is His grace?
What is 'inclusive' anyways?
Are you saying that everyone goes to heaven?
Are you saying that we do not need to make a decision?

The answers to those questions and more are on the way, at least for what I can offer with my limited perspective. For now, I would like to tackle the nature of inclusion to see what is actually being laid out for us in scripture.

THE TICKET

I went on a cruise with my wife for our honeymoon. It was an all-inclusive vacation, which inspired something inside of me regarding the inclusive nature of God's grace. While aboard the ship, we had spent some time eating at the lesser quality restaurants, and had ignored the fine dining in the higher end side because we did not know we could eat there without shelling out a bunch of extra cash. We were going to reserve the nicer dining for an evening together as a special night. On the second day, I went to the guest services desk to find out what my ticket included (we were first time cruise attendees) and was informed that these fine dining restaurants were included in my ticket price. What a good surprise! From then on, we would not eat anywhere else. Why would anyone eat elsewhere when there were personal waiters, fine dining, and as much food as you could handle?

Grace is a lot like that. We do not understand the fullness of the inclusiveness found in grace. We hold the ticket in our hands, which gives us access to the fullness of God's goodness and grace; but some of us wander through life unaware of just how much that ticket includes. Ephesians 2:18-19 tells us of our 'ticket' into the family; therefore, the fullness of God is the person of Jesus Christ.

> **Ephesians 2:18-19** - *For through Him we both have access by one Spirit to the Father. Now, therefore, you are no longer strangers and foreigners, but fellow citizens with the saints and members of the household of God*

Everyone has the same ticket. We are all on board. However, to fully grasp this fact, we need to understand the all-inclusive nature of the law. We have to understand the law included everyone.

> **Romans 5:9-21** - *Much more then, having now been justified by His blood, we shall be saved from wrath through Him. For if when we were enemies we were reconciled to God through the death of His Son, much more, having been reconciled, we shall be saved by His life. And not only that, but we also rejoice in God through our Lord Jesus Christ, through whom we have now received the reconciliation. Therefore, just as through one man sin entered the world, and death through sin, and*

thus death spread to all men, because all sinned-- (For until the law sin was in the world, but sin is not imputed when there is no law. Nevertheless death reigned from Adam to Moses, even over those who had not sinned according to the likeness of the transgression of Adam, who is a type of Him who was to come. But the free gift is not like the offense. For if by the one man's offense many died, much more the grace of God and the gift by the grace of the one Man, Jesus Christ, abounded to many and the gift is not like that which came through the one who sinned. For the judgment, which came from one offense, resulted in condemnation, but the free gift, which came from many offenses, resulted in justification. For if by the one man's offense death reigned through the one, much more those who receive abundance of grace and of the gift of righteousness will reign in life through the One, Jesus Christ.) Therefore, as through one man's offense judgment came to all men, resulting in condemnation, even so through one Man's righteous act the free gift came to all men, resulting in justification of life. For as by one man's disobedience many were made sinners, so also by one Man's obedience many will be made righteous. Moreover the law entered that the offense might abound. But where sin abounded, grace abounded much more, so that as sin reigned in death, even so grace might reign through righteousness to eternal life through Jesus Christ our Lord.

This passage defines it. The law included every man, woman & child from Adam to Christ. It had to. From that time, if anyone could have lived a perfect life apart from Christ, then everyone would have; and Christ's sacrifice would have been unnecessary. We are told in this passage that because of Adam, all people were included in the sin, fall, law, and loss of it all. The fact is we have something so much greater; we were *never* under the law (as ones who have been raised with Him according to Paul in Colossians).

Here lies the problem. We have gone through our Christian lives acting like the law is a better ministry. We have acted as though the law was a more powerful ministry than the ministry of grace. We continue to contend that there are certain ones who are still under the law, and are therefore under the regulation and punishment it offers.

2 Corinthians 3:4-11 - *And we have such trust through Christ toward God. Not that we are sufficient of ourselves to think of anything as being from ourselves, but our sufficiency is from God, who also made us sufficient as ministers of the new covenant, not of the letter but of the Spirit; for the letter kills, but the Spirit gives life. But if the ministry of death, written and engraved on stones, was glorious, so that the children of Israel could not look steadily at the face of Moses because of the* *glory of his countenance, which glory was passing away, how will the ministry of the Spirit not be more glorious? For if the ministry of condemnation had glory, the ministry of righteousness exceeds much more in glory. For even what was made glorious had no glory in this respect, because of the glory that excels. For if what is passing away was glorious, what remains is much more glorious.*

Paul tells us that the ministry of grace (the ministry of righteousness) is greater, more glorious and better than the ministry of death (the ministry of the law).

At this point, I'd like to introduce something I call *contextual math.* Contextual math is a lot like the old form of algebra most of us learned in school. It says this: if x=something and y=something, then x+y=something. This equation suits us nicely when weighing the truths laid out for us in the bible. We should apply it here and see the equation Paul is filling in for us.

If the ministry of death included all people, and the ministry of grace is far better, and still alive, then the *only* conclusion is that the ministry of grace *must* include every man, or it is not the ministry of grace at all! If the message which we are receiving results in a anyone being excluded because of lack of faith, tithing or love; if we are singled out for our sin, or left lacking or rejected in any other area, it is not the ministry of grace!

What is important to understand about the law is that people did not have to confess their belief in the law in order to be subject to it. They could not simply remove themselves from the penalty of the law, or their subjugation to it. They could disobey, and remove themselves from the benefit of obedience; however, they could not choose not to be under it. It was given to all people, whether they liked it or not. Israel were the only ones who followed it, sometimes. But, the whole of humanity fell under its tyrannical rule. In the same fashion, to be under the ministry of God's grace requires nothing of you. We do not have a choice to put ourselves under it or out of it. We cannot pray ourselves into it; we cannot disobey ourselves away from it. We can choose to not participate, but we cannot get away from God's love and grace.

> **1 Timothy 2:1-6** - *Therefore I exhort first of all that supplications, prayers, intercessions, and giving of thanks be made for all men, for kings and all who are in authority, that we may lead a quiet and peaceable life in all godliness and reverence. For this is good and acceptable in the sight of God our Savior, who desires all men to be saved and to come to the knowledge of the truth. For there is one God and one Mediator between God and men, the Man Christ Jesus, who gave Himself a ransom for all, to be testified in due time*

Stay with me on this one, because we need to look at a couple things. Sometimes, we need to dig deeper than the English text. We do not need to be Greek or Hebrew scholars but it is beneficial to *actually* know what was said. I once had a woman ask me why we need to make the bible so complex by always looking into the Greek or Hebrew text. My reply was simple. When looking at a novel, a work of fiction, when we see that a character has walked into a cave, we do not bring out our dictionary to see what walking is and what a cave is. No, due to the nature of the language we speak, we have a picture in our heads. Walking – we see moving legs, man or woman, and cave – we see a dark area, maybe in the side of a mountain, possibly damp, usually full of bats, bugs, and other creepy, crawly things. We have just done a great service to ourselves by allowing our knowledge to paint a fuller picture. Well, in the same light, we need to grasp that our bible was written in Greek, Hebrew, and often spoken in Aramaic. We do not have the Aramaic versions readily available to us (though there are a few). So, we use the Greek and Hebrew lexicons to help us paint a fuller picture of what is being spoken to us through the written word.

Going back to Timothy, just looking at the English in verse 6 *...who gave Himself a ransom for all...* proves my earlier point. Are there any qualifiers here on Christ's sacrifice? NO! Does this verse say *who gave Himself a ransom for those that believe*? NO! It does not leave us with a requirement of 'faith', a requirement of prayer, belief, trust, worship, ceremony, baptism or law.

Just glancing at the final portion of this passage, *to be testified in due time,* it carries with it something enormous, much bigger than we expect from God. The phrasing, *in due time,* means *at the time of crisis.* That is HUGE! Do we understand why that is such a big deal? Most of us do not. Here is yet another spot where we need to dig deeper.

Verse 4 makes this statement ...*who desires all men to be saved and to come to the knowledge of the truth...* This is misleading if we do not understand the truth of salvation! The truth is that salvation was provided the moment Christ was nailed to the cross. In light of that fact, it has been a reality since before we ever accepted our salvation.

In looking at the Greek text, we can see something much greater than our English translators supposed. I want to break this down and illustrate what is really being said here.

- *Who desires* - to take delight in, have pleasure in.
- *All men (people)* - A prevailing doctrine says *all* means *some of all* - however, this word is the same word used when Christ says *man shall not live on bread alone, but by every word....* Did Jesus mean just some of the types of words that come from God? NO! So we cannot change the meaning either. In this context, all means ALL.
- *To be saved* - to keep from danger or destruction, to save a suffering one, to heal, make well, restore to health, rescue, make whole.

So, what is really being said here? *God delights and takes pleasure in the healing, protection, rescuing and wholeness of all people, and delights in their awakening to the truth! For there is one mediator....Christ whose salvation of all will be revealed in times of crisis.* That is bigger than we believe though. Because, after all, God only delights in the healing of those who profess His name.....right? And only when they confess it.....right?

> **1 Timothy 4:10** - *For to this end we both labor and suffer reproach, because we trust in the living God, who is the Savior of all men, especially of those who believe.*

Often times, we forget to read the end of certain verses. This is one of those verses. This is Paul writing to the young pastor whom he left in charge of the church. He is talking about godliness profiting him. We love that verse. We love to tell people it is only by living a Godly life that they will profit, succeed, etc. The world is full of contradictions to this theory, but we preach it anyways. There are millionaires all over the world who never acknowledge God in their lives, never acknowledge His goodness to them; yet they profit. We get around this one by saying "they are not really profiting because they are only rich in money". Well, I am going to be honest. Given the choice, I would much rather be rich than poor. Do I chase down money? No. Do I love money more than God? No. But it is better to have, than to have not.

At any rate, we love that line. We preach 'godliness' but ignore the last part of this verse, because we believe the prior part is *so much more important.* God says this amazing statement through Paul, *Who is the Savior of all men, especially of those who believe.* Wait....savior of all people, especially of those who believe? That sounds like all people are saved. That sounds like all people have been included in the free gift of salvation. That sounds like this doctrine of inclusion that so many run away from. It sounds to me like there is something there, in all people, having included them in this great thing we think *we* have and *they* do not.

Here is the great thing about all of this. Either the gospel includes all people, or it includes *none* of us! If it includes all of us, we have an amazing hope of rescue in times of need. We have the promise of redemption, and a Father who delights to see us get this! So if all people are saved, then everyone is going to heaven right? NO! That is foolish. We think salvation is about heaven and hell....but it is not. However we slice it, *salvation* and *saved* never meant *from hell* or *to heaven.* We have made the bible a heaven and hell issue, which it was never meant to be. It was always meant to be a handbook of relationships. Relationship with each other - love one another – and relationship with God - love the Lord Your God. Heaven is often referred to, but it is almost always as a reference point, never as a destination, and certainly never as a reward for *holy* living.

When we start looking at the truth of all people's inclusion into the salvation message, it changes some things. It makes us honor one another as the family of God, (whether they are estranged or not, they are still family) -

and makes us come to a realization of God's desire for *all people* to live healed, prosperous lives!

Titus 2:11 - *For the grace of God that brings salvation has appeared to all men.*

We have been told that the grace of God has appeared to all people. Again, we usually ignore the whole verse. The natural by-product of God's grace is salvation. We cannot separate the two, but we do. We make grace and salvation two separate things. We say, or think that *God's grace is for everyone, but salvation is only for those who believe.* We believe grace is God's to give; but faith is ours to have. We have learned already that Paul said salvation is for every man, and for those who believe. We need to change our thinking. We need to live like all are just as worthy as those of us who have awakened to our identity as Christ.

Colossians 2:13 - *In Him you were also circumcised with the circumcision made without hands, by putting off the body of the sins of the flesh, by the circumcision of Christ, buried with Him in baptism, in which you also were raised with Him through faith in the working of God, who raised Him from the dead. And you, being dead in your trespasses and the uncircumcision of your flesh, He has made alive together with Him, having forgiven you all trespasses, having wiped out the handwriting of requirements that was* *against us, which was contrary to us. And He has taken it out of the way, having nailed it to the cross. Having disarmed principalities and powers, He made a public spectacle of them, triumphing over them in it. So let no one judge you in food or in drink, or regarding a festival or a new moon or Sabbaths, which are a shadow of things to come, but the substance is of Christ.*

Here is the point. Because of Christ's sacrifice, we were buried and raised with Him; the law has forever been erased over us, or wiped out. It was nailed to the cross. We all love to say amen because it is true! But also, it is true for everyone else. Our main goal as a church is to teach these truths to everyone else. Is there still a need for salvation? - YES!

But it is not what we think.

CALEB MILLER

CHAPTER 5
SAVED, SALVATION, BORN AGAIN

"I have come that they may have life"
John 10:10

W E ARE THE ONES WHO have made salvation into a heaven and hell issue, not God. Salvation is something God bestowed upon man, a way of restoring all that Adam lost and more. It is a way of adoption into the Family of God that Jesus provided for all humanity. (Adoption, culturally speaking, is both the process by which an illegitimate child becomes a legitimate one, as well as the process by which a blood born child is ushered into adulthood.) We know what religion has allowed us to know of salvation. This leaves us in a place of lack and cannot be the ministry of grace. Religion takes a beautiful gift from God, whittles it down to a sharpened stick and brings death by beating us to a bloody pulp!

So what is salvation all about?
If salvation is not about heaven and hell, how do we get to heaven?
Just how do we obtain salvation?

Those are important questions, especially in light of the last few thoughts we discussed about grace, and briefly about salvation. It is something we need to grasp as believers in order to lead others into a true revelation of what Jesus Christ is really all about - abundant life; and to minister the only way Paul told us to minister – reconciliatory.

SALVATION

First, we should talk about *salvation* and see what it really means.

> **Romans 10:4-13** *For Christ is the end of the law for righteousness to everyone who believes. For Moses writes about the righteousness, which is of the law, "The man who does those things shall live by them." But the righteousness of faith speaks in this way, "Do not say in your heart, 'Who will ascend into heaven?'" (that is, to bring Christ*

down from above) or, "'who will descend into the abyss?'" (that is, to bring Christ up from the dead). But what does it say? "The word is near you, in your mouth and in your heart" (that is, the word of faith which we preach): that if you confess with your mouth the Lord Jesus and believe in your heart that God has raised Him from the dead, you will be saved. For with the heart one believes unto righteousness, and with the mouth confession is made unto salvation. For the Scripture says, "Whoever believes on Him will not be put to shame." For there is no distinction between Jew and Greek, for the same Lord over all is rich to all who call upon Him. For "whoever calls on the name of the LORD shall be saved."

This would seem to be the definitive verse about salvation. It is part of the 'Romans Road' we are taught in youth camp. You know, the time of our lives when we are told our 'duty to God' is to make mass converts of the world. What I find funny about what most Christians spend their lives doing is not at all what Christ told us to do. Christ told us to go into all the world and make disciples (Matt 28:19), to heal the sick, raise the dead, cast out devils (Matt 10:8) and to love our neighbors (Matt 22:39). What is so amazing about those three instructions from Christ is that they are the summation of salvation's true message. Before we get into what salvation really means, we will take a brief sidetrack into what the bible says about how to 'gain' salvation.

In looking at this passage in Romans, there are actually two 'methods' to receiving salvation.

1. *Confess with your mouth the Lord Jesus & believe in your heart God raised Him from the dead* (notice it does not say confess with your mouth & believe in your heart. It actually separates those two things. God does not require our faith to match our speech. Our hearts can always believe more than our mouths can say).

2. *Whoever calls upon the name of the Lord will be saved.* (again, notice there is no requirement of faith here).

So, according to Romans, it is either confession of Jesus Christ, or calling upon the name of the Lord. So all I have to do is say "GOD"?

Luke 19:8-9 *Then Zacchaeus stood and said to the Lord, "Look, Lord, I give half of my goods to the poor; and if I have taken anything from anyone by false accusation, I restore fourfold." And Jesus said to him, "Today salvation has come to this house, because he also is a son of Abraham"*

So again, we see two different roads to salvation. Either Zack is saved because of how much he gave to the poor or because of his nationality. So is there any hope for those of us who are cheap, stingy Americans?

Romans 1:16 - *For I am not ashamed of the gospel of Christ, for it is the power of God to salvation for everyone who believes, for the Jew first and also for the Greek*

AHA! It is our belief again. That must be the answer.

Right?

Romans 13:11 - *And do this, knowing the time, that now it is high time to awake out of sleep; for now our salvation is nearer than when we first believed.*

If our belief brings salvation, then Paul would not have said it is *nearer than when we first believed.* So is it an ongoing belief then?

2 Corinthians 7:10 - *For godly sorrow produces repentance leading to salvation, not to be regretted; but the sorrow of the world produces death.*

Here it is.... Our repentance brings salvation. Never mind what we have just studied on it being our confession, how much we give, our nationality, our belief or our faith. We have taken this verse and made it the key to salvation. I want to take a break here and look at what is really being said in this verse.

The phrase 'Godly sorrow' could not be further from the intended meaning. Its real meaning is this: *the sorrow which comes down from God Himself* - meaning, the broken heart of God when His son was nailed to the cross is what brings the mind change needed to receive salvation. That is a bit different and so it takes our repentance right out of the picture again!

2 Thessalonians 2:13 - *But we are bound to give thanks to God always for you, brethren beloved by the Lord, because God from the beginning chose you for salvation through sanctification by the Spirit and belief in the truth*

This changes everything because according to Paul God chose us for salvation - from the beginning. So since it is not our faith, color, belief, repentance or confession - is it God's choice of us?

Hebrews 5:9 - *And having been perfected, He became the author of eternal salvation to all who obey Him,*

Or is it our obedience?

Well, what is the point of all this? All of these things sum up to one main point: reception and acceptance. Our receiving and accepting salvation makes it real to us and gets us to a point of having the fullness of this stuff active in our lives. God is far more concerned *that* we get it rather than *how* we get it. He knows much better than we do that getting to know Him produces the fruit called belief for which we are searching.

Ok, so that is the *how*...now for the *what*.

What does salvation mean? Again, we need to look at the actual definition from the Greek text. *Salvation: deliverance, preservation, safety, salvation – deliverance from the molestation of enemies – in an ethical sense, that which concludes to the soul's safety or salvation – salvation as the present possession of all true Christians – future salvation, the sum of benefits and blessings which the Christians, redeemed from all earthly ills, will enjoy after the visible return of Christ from heaven in the consummated and eternal kingdom of God.*

Whew! That encompasses quite a bit. But look at this – deliverance, preservation & safety! This is a message of 'set free from the past, present and future!' It is exactly what Christ said – abundant life. Our *salvation* is a message always intended to free us from the bonds of our past, preserve our well being for today, and guarantee that same well being for tomorrow. Look at the fourth definition again, salvation as the *present* possession and redeemed from *all* earthly ills! And that is just the definition of the word *salvation.*

God's design and plan is to take care of us from start to finish. Our choices do not negate the gift; they do not remove it from us. They do not even remove us from our worth to receive it. We must understand the nature of the working of God. We can only do what He has already done for us. Because He has accepted us, we are saying, we must and can now accept.

SAVED

Ok, so *salvation* means all of that, but what about *saved?* As we dig into the Greek text for the word *saved,* surely we will find this heaven and hell issue Christianity has made such a major focus.

Saved in the Greek means: *to save, keep safe and sound, to rescue from danger or destruction one (from injury or peril) to save a suffering one (from perishing), i.e. one suffering from disease, to make well, heal, restore to health to preserve one who is in danger of destruction.*

Much like *salvation, saved* has some differences. In the book of Matthew, Jesus tells us *he who endures to the end* is who will be saved (Matt 10:22 & 24:13). So, if we endure then it is for sure...well...maybe we should look at that through the finished work of Christ. After all, we have to understand Christ as a teacher ministering to the house of Israel. If it is only he who endures till the end who is saved, and Christ endured for us, and He lives in us, then we are those who endure till the end. Meaning - we are saved! Then, we have Mark 16, which tells us, he who believes and is baptized will be saved. Then, there is Luke 7:50 where Jesus tells the woman that her faith has saved her.

There are countless scriptures with countless ways to be saved. What we need to understand, and what is key to all of this is that *salvation* and *saved* are two DIFFERENT things!

Salvation is God's free gift to all people. Being saved is experiencing more of the FULLNESS of salvation once the acceptance has been made. This is where the acceptance, profession, and belief of Christ as Lord come into play. This is where we have to make that decision. Our faith in Christ's faith brings the already present salvation into reality, thereby rendering us *saved*. We have to look at things from the Father's eternal perspective. He has absolute faith in the power and completion of His Son's work. He has absolute faith that it was enough for all mankind. From His point of view, we have been saved. The nature of standing outside of time though allows for all to be saved, and still *get saved*. However, if we are going to take a dogmatic approach to people *getting saved*, then we need to take the whole thing into context.

Romans 10:9 - *that if you confess with your mouth the Lord Jesus and believe in your heart that God has raised Him from the dead, you will be saved.*

This is the typical argument for *getting saved*. However, Philippians has something to say about this.

Philippians 2:9-11 - *Therefore God also has highly exalted Him and given Him the name which is above every name that at the name of*

*Jesus every knee should bow, of those in heaven,
and of those on earth, and of those under the earth
and [that] every tongue should confess that Jesus
Christ [is] Lord, to the glory of God the Father*

So if we stay with our dogma about Romans, then according to Paul's letter, everyone is saved. If the typical religious mantra of "confession and belief" is what it is all about, then according to Paul, since everyone will confess, everyone is saved. But if we will get beyond our dogma and fear, we will discover it is about something else.

We are told in 1 Corinthians 12:3 *Therefore I make known to you that no one speaking by the Spirit of God calls Jesus accursed, and no one can say that Jesus is Lord except by the Holy Spirit.*

Only by the Holy Spirit can one say Jesus is Lord. This means the Spirit has to be there with us already. We have this belief that the Spirit comes when we make the confession, but according to Paul, it is just the opposite. Our confession comes because the Spirit is already there! What does this mean for our typical approach to getting people "into the kingdom"? This means Jesus did the work! He brought us all into the kingdom once and for all. I am sure religion is welling up in you now, but stay with me on this.

We HAVE to change our belief about what salvation is. We have just learned salvation is deliverance, preservation, safety - this leads to something. Salvation is about freedom and freedom is only necessary where oppression exists. Oppression does not exist in heaven; so freedom and salvation are about life right now! The same can be said for 'saved'.

What we are missing in all of this is the truth and we have to understand that "every good and perfect gift comes down from the Father" (James 1:17). Therefore, anyone who is experiencing health, prosperity, freedom, etc. is experiencing the fruit of the salvation God gave freely to all humanity. They are not experiencing the fullness though! That is where acceptance comes into play.

When we accept Jesus' work, we begin to see the fullness of what Christ provided. Acceptance is ONLY necessary for fullness, not to make the free gift somehow magically manifest. It is already here!

If we are going to say that those who do not experience the fullness are not "saved", then 100% of the church today is unsaved! However, if we will begin to change our speech to say that it is no longer about "saved" or "unsaved" but is now about "believer" and "unbeliever" then, we will see something begin to happen. We all walk in different areas of unbelief in our lives. Yet we would not say we are not saved. The same applies to the world at large. People were all saved by the finished work of Christ; they just have not awakened or opened their eyes yet. They have not accepted their invitation to the table of the Lord.

THE FIREMAN

If a fireman was to pull someone from a burning building, and that person sat on the ground with their eyes closed expecting the fire to come, what they would experience is sheer hell and unbelief. But, if they opened their eyes to the rescue that already took place, they would begin to rejoice in their freedom and peace! This world is full of those people who have been rescued from the fire, but have not yet opened their eyes. We are called to help them open their eyes to the truth of their ALREADY PROVIDED rescue! Not to tell them they are burning!

The truth of it all is none of this is about heaven or hell. It is about what Paul said in Ephesians.

I read this with great joy, because it is the single biggest truth in the word! Here is the man who spent several years alone with Christ in the wilderness, learning and being taught by the one who did it all and he makes this marvelous statement:

Ephesians 1:7-10 (PHILLIPS) - *It is through the Son, at the cost of his own blood, that we are redeemed, freely forgiven through that full and generous grace which has overflowed into our lives and opened our eyes to the truth. For God had allowed us to know the secret of his plan, and it is this:*

(I am going to break in here. To me, when I see the man who spent this time alone with Christ, make the statement "the secret of God's plan" - it jumps out at me as something of which I should really take note. This just may be the single most important thing in the bible.)

Continued - *He purposes in his sovereign will that all human history shall be consummated in Christ, that everything that exists in Heaven or earth shall find its perfection and fulfillment in him.*

He purposes in HIS SOVEREIGN WILL that ALL HUMAN HISTORY shall be consummated in Christ! (Sorry for the all caps, but it is just that exciting!) *Consummated* means to be brought to a place of oneness. Think about the marriage metaphor. When a newly married couple consummates their marriage, the two become one. Interestingly too, up until the recent era, until a marriage had been consummated, it was not a legal marriage and could still be annulled! Christ consummated the whole of human history, past to future, so that we would be one with Him! That oneness is something we just do not grasp. We are at a place of unity with the Son and the Father.

Look at Psalm 22 - we know this is a prophetic Psalm about Jesus, "my God, my God, why have you forsaken me?" But what we do not do is look to the rest of the passage to see what the end result of the Crucifixion of our Savior was meant to accomplish. Look at verse 27:

Psalm 22:27 - *All the ends of the world Shall remember and turn to the LORD, And all the families of the nations Shall worship before You.*

All the ends of the world shall remember and turn to the Lord? But we keep on teaching that our confession and belief saves us. Nope, His faith saved us, His work provided all of this, and His avenue of adoption made it a reality.

The truth of this is that Jesus was sent for our adoption, to usher us back into a place of oneness with the Father, Son and Holy Spirit, and there are those out there with their eyes closed to that fact, some in the world and others in the church. They do not know what He did, because there has been a fear of words, fear of man, fear of peers, and fear of judgment.

BORN AGAIN

I am utterly astonished at how this particular terminology has become so deeply engrained in the minds and hearts of those who would proclaim Christianity. Born again is something that occurs a mere three times in the entirety of the bible, twice spoken by Jesus and once by Peter.

> John 3:3 - *Jesus answered and said to him, "Most assuredly, I say to you, unless one is born again, he cannot see the kingdom of God."*

Jesus is not giving us some new requirement of belief. However, He is giving us a preview of His intention. He is saying here - *if you want to see God, I need to bear you in me, so you can be born again - as a new man.* Most of us understand the words *born again* mean something like *born of God.* Also, there is an understated meaning to *again* - it is *from the beginning*. That brings something to mind: if Jesus was the lamb slain from the foundation of the world (or the beginning) and He has said He is about to make us all born from the beginning - then we are something different. We are born in Him, from the foundation of the world, as sons of the Father! Jesus is telling us that He is about to push reset for us. He is going to take us all the way back to the beginning, before Adam was even created as a being - to the place where He was with God, living as God's Son, and put us there with Him.

Do we understand what this means? Was there sickness at God's side before man came to being? Was there poverty? Was there fear? Was there doubt? Was there pain, shame, grief, strife or death? NO! There was only God living freely with none of the weights of this world in relationship with His family. Now, because of Christ's work, mankind has been born back to that place.

God sent His Son to push reset for us. We need to reset our thinking, reset our lives, and go back to the place the manufacturer set up for us to be at optimum running speed and performance!

"WITHOUT EXCUSE"

One of the typical offerings about people who have never heard about the Father and His love is a passage from Romans where Paul tells the people who are disguising the truth with lies that they are without excuse. Without going too deeply into the context of the verse, we ought to look quickly at this belief and see why it is so poisonous.

If we are to believe the necessary road to salvation is confession and belief in Christ, as the bible tells us, then we cannot hold a doctrine of "without excuse". If a man or woman is working in the field and they begin to look heavenward and somehow come to the realization that there must have been some sort of creator God who made all this, then, how are they to logically make the jump that this creator God sent His only Son, who died for their *sins*, and rose again, and then somehow make the jump to confession of that Son's sacrifice? How then are they to make the assumption, according to some traditions, that they must then be baptized, and filled with the Holy Spirit? Religion would like to say, "I would like to believe God will send someone". That is all well and good, but what you would like to believe and the truth are often two separate things!

This is not the grace of God; it is the explaining away of religion. Either we believe salvation comes through belief in Christ alone, or we do not. If we do, we need to say sorry to those people because according to our professed and vocalized beliefs, they will be in hell forever. However, if we can change our view of salvation, we can open our eyes to further grace and a deeper revelation of the Father's love.

It is sometimes easy for us to lose sight of recent history. With the advent of things like Facebook, twitter, email, and the ease of information exchange, we see things almost instantly. This was not true for so long though. Just looking backward to American history we see a people group living on the continent, away from missionaries, away from information exchange, away from any knowledge of the religious "God" of the Europeans – the American Indians. Are we to say that they were *without excuse* for not believing in a God they had never heard of, not jumping to His Son they had never been introduced to, and not making the association of the forgiveness of their *sins*? These are questions we need to ponder!

CALEB MILLER

CHAPTER 6
FOODS THAT PROFIT NOTHING

"All the world is made of faith, and trust, and pixie dust."
J.M. Barrie, Peter Pan

I KNOW THAT JUST THE title of this chapter may have encouraged a mass book burning in certain areas of the globe. Please stay with me on this; it is not as bad as you might think. In order to get off this ride that religion has us on, we need to redefine much of our terminology. We need to adjust our semantics, and see what the real truth is behind some of the terms we hold so dearly. There are no two words that mean more to the heart of Christendom than the words *grace* and *faith*. We hold dearly to our faith, to what we believe, and that this belief is brought by grace.

There are few subjects among Christians that are as sacred and touchy as the topic of faith. Is it God's faith, my faith, a combination of both, neither, or all of the above? We have been taught, "without faith it is impossible to please God" (which in turn inspires in me the question of "so with faith is it only *possible* to please Him?"), and that faith is what saves us, whether it is what we put our faith in, or how great or little it is. We have been taught that faith is the opposite of fear, even though we are told that perfect love is what casts out fear, and that faith is our necessary response. I want to tread lightly because I know this is a serious subject, and one that if treated with disrespect can cause great problems for the hearer. So hunker down, buckle up, and prepare to take a ride through the word and see what we find.

First we need to look at the very word we have made into an action on our behalf - faith - *pistis*, which is a feminine NOUN! If faith were a verb, requiring action on our part, then we could just stop right here! But it is not, and so we must study it out. We use phrases like *he or she is a man or woman of faith!* Usually what is implied by this is that they are a person of action or power. That could be the case if faith were a verb, but with it being a noun, that is akin to saying *he or she is a person of pizza!*

In our English translations we have lost something simple. Most often it is a small two-letter word change that we skim right over, yet without proper understanding of the literal text, changes everything! We are going to look at the fact that nearly every time the word *faith* is used in reference to what we possess (as opposed to *in the faith* - as in our religion), we see something subtle that has been introduced through years of tradition. There is a lot of scripture coming, so hunker down!

Galatians 2:16 - *knowing that a man is not justified by the works of the law but by faith in Jesus Christ, even we have believed in Christ Jesus, that we might be justified by faith in Christ and not by the works of the law; for by the works of the law no flesh shall be justified.*

KJV - *Knowing that a man is not justified by the works of the law, but by the faith of Jesus Christ, even we have believed in Jesus Christ, that we might be justified by the faith of Christ, and not by the works of the law: for by the works of the law shall no flesh be justified.*

Galatians 3:26 - *For you are all sons of God through faith in Christ Jesus*

YLT - *for ye are all sons of God through the faith in Christ Jesus* (in the Greek, *the faith that is found in Christ.)*

Philippians 3:8-9 - *Yet indeed I also count all things loss for the excellence of the knowledge of Christ Jesus my Lord, for whom I have suffered the loss of all things, and count them as rubbish, that I may gain Christ and be found in Him, not having my own* *righteousness, which is from the law, but that which is through faith in Christ, the righteousness which is from God by faith.*

KJV - *Yea doubtless, and I count all things but loss for the excellency of the knowledge of Christ Jesus my Lord: for whom I have suffered the loss of all things, and do count them but dung, that I may win Christ, And be found in him, not having mine own righteousness, which is of the law, but that which is through the faith of Christ, the righteousness which is of God by faith.*

Colossians 1:4 - *since we heard of your faith in Christ Jesus and of your love for all the saints.*

YLT - *having heard of your faith in Christ Jesus, and of the love that [is] to all the saints,*

Colossians 2:5 - *For though I am absent in the flesh, yet I am with you in spirit, rejoicing to see your good order and the steadfastness of your faith in Christ.*

YLT - *for if even in the flesh I am absent -- yet in the spirit I am with you, joying and beholding your order, and the steadfastness of your faith in regard to Christ*

Romans 3:22 - *even the righteousness of God, through faith in Jesus Christ, to all and on all[a] who believe. For there is no difference.*

KJV - *Even the righteousness of God which is by faith of Jesus Christ unto all and upon all them that believe: for there is no difference.*

Galatians 2:20 - *I have been crucified with Christ; it is no longer I who live, but Christ lives in me; and the life which I now live in the flesh I live by faith in the Son of God, who loved me and gave Himself for me.*

KJV - *I am crucified with Christ: nevertheless I live; yet not I, but Christ liveth in me: and the life which I now live in the flesh I live by the faith of the Son of God, who loved me, and gave himself for me.*

Galatians 3:14 - *that the blessing of Abraham might come upon the Gentiles in Christ Jesus, that we might receive the promise of the Spirit through faith.*

YLT - *that to the nations the blessing of Abraham may come in Christ Jesus, that the promise of the Spirit we may receive through the faith*

Galatians 3:22 - *But the Scripture has confined all under sin, that the promise by faith in Jesus Christ might be given to those who believe.*

YLT - *but the Writing did shut up the whole under sin, that the promise by faith of Jesus Christ may be given to those believing.*

Ephesians 3:17a - *that Christ may dwell in your hearts through faith*

YLT - *that the Christ may dwell through the faith in your hearts*

1 Thessalonians 1:3 - *remembering without ceasing your work of faith, labor of love, and patience of hope in our Lord Jesus Christ in the sight of our God and Father*

YLT - *unceasingly remembering of you the work of the faith, and the labour of the love, and the endurance of the hope, of our Lord Jesus Christ, in the presence of our God and Father*

1 Timothy 1:14 - *And the grace of our Lord was exceedingly abundant, with faith and love which are in Christ Jesus*

KJV - *And the grace of our Lord was exceeding abundant with faith and love which is in Christ Jesus.*

1 Timothy 3:13b - *and great boldness in the faith which is in Christ Jesus.*

2 Timothy 1:13 - *Hold fast the pattern of sound words which you have heard from me, in faith and love which are in Christ Jesus. The KJV uses is in Christ, signifying singleness rather than separation.*

2 Timothy 3:15 - *and that from childhood you have known the Holy Scriptures, which are able to make you wise for salvation through faith which is in Christ Jesus.*

This is quite exhaustive, but necessary. What we see from looking into all of these passages is that faith is ALWAYS referred to as being found *in* Christ or being *of* Christ. Faith as a noun is something He possesses and bears in us. Faith is produced by the fact that we are *in* Christ. The translators (mostly of the KJV to NKJV) wrongly substituted that one little word *in* for the literal *of,* forever changing how the world views faith!

SAVING FAITH

We have some understanding of something we call *saving faith* - that faith which ushers us into salvation. But again, is this a scriptural belief?

James 2:14 - *What does it profit, my brethren, if someone says he has faith but does not have works? Can faith save him?*

The understood answer to James' question here is no! This faith that a man has alone cannot save him! What is James really saying then? He is telling us that if a man says that *he* has faith, then that same man would be able to do something - works. Jesus was the only one who could have possessed and worked faith - and so He did. If faith could

97

have saved us then it would have! It is the same thing we use to apply the perfection rule. If anyone could have lived perfectly, then they would have, and Jesus' fulfillment of the law would be unnecessary. His sacrifice would remain, but for different reasons, adoption and remission of something else.

FOODS THAT PROFIT NOTHING

Hebrews 11-13 - Without going fully into Hebrews 11 I want to briefly look at what the writer says in regards to faith.

This whole chapter is about the heroes of faith from the Old Testament. By faith, so and so did this or that. From Abel to Jericho, encompassing the heroes of faith in the Jewish history. By faith, by faith, by faith! And yet in V39-40 we find the summary of this passage:

> **Hebrews 11:39-40** - *And all these, having obtained a good testimony through faith, did not receive the promise, God having provided something better for us, that they should not be made perfect apart from us.*

Regardless of their faith, they still did not receive the promise! We just saw this same truth from James. Faith could not save them, they did not get the promise - however necessary their faith was, it was unable to save! Context demands that we go further to see a bigger picture.

Hebrews 12:1-2 YLT - *Therefore, we also having so great a cloud of witnesses set around us, every weight having put off, and the closely besetting sin, through endurance may we run the contest that is set before us, looking to the author and perfecter of faith -- Jesus, who, over-against the joy set before him -- did endure a cross, shame having despised, on the right hand also of the throne of God did sit down;*

The text from John's gospel *"In the beginning was the word, and the word was with God, and the word was God"* in this passage from Hebrews becomes *Jesus, the author of faith.* Not only is He the *word* of God, but He is also the author of faith. And not only is He the author of faith, He is the perfecter (read: finisher) of it. We need to understand something that is not written on the pages of the book. Namely, that faith is required to be perfect. The only faith that accomplishes anything is perfect faith. This is not condemnation or a call to self-examination - it is hope! Jesus tells us in Matthew to be perfect as our Father is perfect, but what He is saying is that *you shall be perfect.* He is giving us a preview of what He is here to do. He was here to perfect us, and to perfect that which He authored - faith. Faith has been made perfect through the man Jesus Christ. Other versions say the finisher of faith, and that is also true. He is the last one who could have ever had faith. It was His to possess from the beginning, His to author, His to finish, His to perfect. I will finalize this portion with a strong statement from the author of Hebrews.

> **Hebrews 13:9** - *Do not be carried about with various and strange doctrines. For it is good that the heart be established by grace, not with foods which have not profited those who have been occupied with them.*

What has the author just spent all this time talking about? Faith (the kind that we have)! What is he/she saying here? That to be occupied with our own faith in any form is "food that profits nothing". This is a strong statement, and one that is completely contradictory to what the church teaches today. We are told that our faith is to do this or that, but the author is telling us that this same faith profits nothing! We are to be established in GRACE!

Is grace just some new work? Is it something that bears fruit in us of "godly living"? No! Godly living is not some *litmus test* by which we can tell if someone is really *under grace.* Grace says no matter how you live, you are justified in life - by the Man, Christ Jesus!

So how then is faith applicable to our lives today?

FAITH AS FRUIT

Something that God began birthing in me recently is this phrase: *Faith is no longer a prerequisite to knowing Him; it is a byproduct of it.* This may be hard to swallow at first because we have been wrongly taught that you confess by faith, then Jesus comes down on his flying carpet into your heart, then you can get to know Him. Well, once again, let us see what the bible says:

Hebrews 11:1 - *Now faith is the substance of things hoped for, the evidence of things not seen.*

I want to remove some words to see what the author is saying. *Now faith is the evidence.* You see, *then* faith was the prerequisite, but *now* faith is the product! Faith is a fruit!

Romans 10:17 - *So then faith comes by hearing, and hearing by the word of God.*

We can use math here. As in all equations, there is a way to prove the answer. With multiplication you divide, with addition you subtract. The proof happens by reversing the answer. Doing this with Romans 10:17 we get the Word gives hearing, and hearing gives faith. Who is the word? JESUS CHRIST! In this passage *word* is *rhema*, not *logos* which is what John uses to name Jesus, but we need to grasp that *rhema* comes from The Logos – who is Christ. *Rhema* does not come from *gramma* (writings/scripture) or *graphe* (writings/scripture) but by *logos* - the speech, or decree of the revelation of God, the man Christ Jesus.

2 Peter 1:3 - *as His divine power has given to us all things that [pertain] to life and godliness, through the knowledge of Him who called us by glory and virtue,*

Peter lines this out for us very well. Through the knowledge of Him (Christ), His divine power has given to us all things = *Knowledge produces all things (of which faith is a part).* Jesus deals with faith twice by referencing it to a mustard seed. Typically we take an approach of "as small as a mustard seed" being the size of faith we need to accomplish great things. Again, we owe it to ourselves to dig on in and see what Jesus is saying, by first keeping in mind that He is here for who? (The lost sheep of the house of Israel.) This means that He is speaking to Jews about things with Jewish customs in mind.

Matthew 13:31-32 - *Another parable He put forth to them, saying: The kingdom of heaven is like a mustard seed, which a man took and sowed in his field, which indeed is the least of all the seeds; but when it is grown it is greater than the herbs and becomes a tree, so that the birds of the air come and nest in its branches.*

Remember, in every parable we need to understand two things: First, that the *man or woman* is always the Father. Second, that the next statement always refers to humanity or the world. So, in this parable, the kingdom of heaven is like a mustard seed, which the Father took and sowed into this earth, into humanity. What is important about this? Well, remember that Jesus is speaking to people who largely had the Old Testament memorized, especially the laws and customs. Even if they did not have them memorized, many at least had a working knowledge of the biblical guidelines and especially the sacrificial animals. His speaking of the birds nesting in the branches of this mustard plant speaks volumes to them that we do not understand without looking back.

We will not go fully into these passages for the sake of time (and immense boredom digging through the book of Leviticus), but here are the references to some of what the birds were to the Jews.

- **Leviticus 14:3-7** - the sanctification and declaration of cleanliness of lepers by the sacrificing of one bird, using another to declare the man clean, then releasing it into the wilderness to carry his disease away.
- **Leviticus 48-53** - The same process, only this time for a whole household.
- **Leviticus 12:6-8** - Birds used in sacrifice to declare a new mother clean after her flow of blood has stopped.
- **Genesis 8:11** - The Dove sent out of the Ark to see if the waters had receded - in essence proof of safety.

- **Genesis 15:9** - God tells Abram to bring a pigeon and a turtledove and uses the whole sacrifice to make a promise of his inheritance among the nations.

So, to the Jew a bird is their declaration of healing, declaration of forgiveness of sins, declaration of cleanliness, declaration of safety, and declaration of inheritance. And what is better about all of this is that the leper did not have to believe in his cleanliness, the priest merely needed to declare it. The same can be said for the home, cleanliness etc. How does this tie back to the parable though? If the *man* is the Father, and the field is this earth, humanity, what did the Father sow? Jesus Christ! He sowed His Son into this earth, which is a small thing to the eyes of man, born in a stable, to a carpenter. Yet when He grew into that which He was destined to be (the Savior of all mankind) the *birds* came back from the wilderness to find rest in His branches. Our healing, cleanliness, remission of sin, safety, and inheritance is found in Him! Taking that forward a bit, understanding that Jesus is this mustard seed, we now go to Matthew 17:20.

Matthew 17:20 - *if you have faith as a mustard seed, you will say to this mountain, 'Move from here to there,' and it will move; and nothing will be impossible for you.*

Notice quickly, Jesus does not say *if you had faith in a mustard seed.* He says faith *as* a mustard seed. Who is the mustard seed? Christ! Jesus is not setting them up for failure! He is setting the stage for what faith really is. It is the person of Christ. If you had what I am, you could say. The implied statement is *because you do not have*. And the only way we can ever *have* is to begin to get to know Him better. Knowing Him produces faith in us.

I would like to close this chapter with this little illustration. If I were to call my wife, and to ask her to do something for me (within reason) I have total *faith* that she will do what I have asked. Why? Because I *know* my wife! If I did not know her intimately, my request would result in, at best, a *wish* that she would do what I asked. Since I know her, faith is a product of our relationship. I do not have to wish that she would do something, or even to hope that she would, I can have faith. This is where we must arrive. Rather than studying faith, pursuing healing and chasing after riches, we should rather do something Jesus said, and that is *"seek first His kingdom"* or *"seek Him"*. We need to get to know Him, and all these things will be added unto us!

Another way to look at this is how I like to diagram the gospel. Everything in the bible stems from one of two trees. There is the tree of the knowledge of good and evil, which is the tree of separation (when we believe we can distinguish good from evil, we are ministers of separation, or serpent ministers) and the tree of life, the tree of reconciliation. The cross of Christ is this tree. Jesus is our reconciliation. His life, death and resurrection are the foundation upon which the gospel is laid, and the ministry we have been given according to Paul is the ministry of reconciliation.

Everything stems from these two trees. Either we are ministering separation, and allowing it to bear its fruit – fruit we see rampant in the Old Testament, or we are ministering reconciliation and allowing it to bear its fruit. What is the fruit of reconciliation? See this diagram to understand it a little more clearly, but everything we pursue in this life we call *Christian* is meant to be a fruit of abiding in the vine, Christ. The fruit will bear itself if we have the correct seed, so if we are not seeing the fruit we think we ought to be, it would make sense to change the seed! I certainly could never *worship, pray, have faith, or give* in order to change an apple into a banana! I would have to plant a banana tree instead!

RECONCILIATION

caleb miller

CALEB MILLER

CHAPTER 7

THE ELEPHANT IN THE ROOM

"I know you don't like it but now listen my friend, just cause you don't like it doesn't mean it's a sin"
Don Francisco, Freedom to Move

NOW THAT WE HAVE a proper understanding of grace and faith, we can begin to address things that have been the primary focus of religion. Religion would like to have us focus primarily on ourselves instead of Christ. And, there is no bigger focus than the subject of sin, another *hold you on the ground* doctrine that proclaims, "your actions must line up" (with whoever it is that makes these rules). If we have sin in our life, we cannot possibly expect God to heal, provide for, or even come live in us. And heaven forbid we die with sin in our life. For this, we will be banished for eternity to be burned but not consumed...to pull our skin off, gnash our teeth until they shatter, and be tormented by Satan, the very being who was supposedly defeated at the cross....but he will have power again at the end of time, right?

Does this sound like a loving God? If a man were convicted of half the things we attribute to God, no mindset in the world would free him from the death penalty. We should get into it though, because it needs to be discussed.

Romans 6:23 - *For the wages of sin is death, but the gift of God is eternal life in Christ Jesus our Lord.*

This is the verse religion uses. We have all heard and have been abused by it. We have all been made subject to the whim of the religious leader who tells us exactly which sin it is that really causes death in our lives. We have been taught the 'sin' of _____ is the one that will kill our relationship, our soul, and us. We have been beaten up and told that our particular brand of failure is the abomination that will kill us all. This is a lie! The truth in this verse is so much more than what we have been taught by the masters of manipulation.

What is a wage? It is a payment for work done, or a due. So we can deconstruct this verse to say, the payment for the work done by sin is death, but the gift of God is life. What did Isaiah say again?

Isaiah 40:2 - *Speak comfort to Jerusalem, and cry out to her, That her warfare is ended, That her*

*iniquity is pardoned; For she has received from the
LORD's hand Double for all her sins."*

DOUBLE!!! This verse is a prophecy of Christ's
payment. It is not enough that we have been taught our sin
has not even been pardoned. It is not enough that we have
been told we have to confess our sin, deal with it and stand
up in front of the congregation, but we have not been told
the truth. Not only did Christ pay for our sin, HE PAID
DOUBLE!!! A double payment ensures the due will never
again be required. (I should interject here that Jesus was not
"paying" the devil as a rightful owner, neither was He
"paying" the Father in a transactional sacrifice. His
"payment" for our sin was in taking the result of our sin upon
Himself, and revealing a heart of peace in the midst of such
great pain).

As if that is not enough, God paid, but He also gave a
free gift, the gift of salvation. The truth is that the GIFT -
the free, unmerited (unearned, unable to be worked for), gift
of God is eternal life in Christ Jesus. God gave us a gift of
eternal life. A gift given by God does not get withdrawn
because we neglected to acknowledge the gift, forgot to pray
a prayer of salvation or did not realize what we had.

Romans 11:29 - *For the gifts and the calling of
God are irrevocable.*

So here we have it. The gift of God is eternal life in
Christ Jesus, and according to Paul, the gift of God is

irrevocable. This means that God will never remove His gift, He will never repent of His gift, nor will He take it back. This has to challenge our typical theology.

I know I am challenging the norm. I know I am shifting your thinking. I know you will probably put this book down several times, and take it back up again to see where I am going next. Keep reading.

As if Isaiah's prophecy was not enough, Paul gives us another answer. Remember 2 Corinthians 5:14? Let us read further in that verse.

2 Corinthians 5:14 - *For the love of Christ compels us, because we judge thus: that if One died for all, then all died.*

The wages of sin was death, but according to Paul, we already died. Remember what Paul said in Colossians 3:11 - that Christ is *in* all? All people had to be in Christ at His death and resurrection, or anyone not born at the time of the greatest single act of love mankind has ever known would be excluded. To be *in* Christ, is to have Christ *in* you. His fellowship is mutual indwelling, and cannot be tossed aside. This passage is so full of the love of God, so full of the truth of the gospel, and so full of grace that to ignore these truths is to say we do not want the truth … this grace is just too far for me. God could not possibly include *them*. Because after all it makes us feel better to know there are those who will not make it. It makes us feel more special to know we will one day look down from heaven on all the billions of people who died and never prayed a "sinner's prayer" – to watch them forever be tormented in hell, a place so terrifying that the very name is used to talk of fear and flame.

Read this carefully because I want this to be clear. The law was not given in order to show anyone his or her need of God, to protect humanity so Christ could be born or to give man something to attain to in order to achieve holiness. The law was given for one reason: that SIN should abound! I know that is a large statement and hard to accept; but I want us look together at something.

> **Romans 5:18-21** - *Therefore, as through one man's offense [judgment came] to all men, resulting in condemnation, even so through one Man's righteous act [the free gift came] to all men, resulting in justification of life. For as by one man's disobedience many were made sinners, so also by one Man's obedience many will be made righteous. Moreover the law entered that the offense might abound. But where sin abounded, grace abounded much more, so that as sin reigned in death, even so grace might reign through righteousness to eternal life through Jesus Christ our Lord.*

Verse 20 clearly states what I was saying. *The law entered that the offense might abound.* The law simply was not there to show man anything, but rather to increase sin. And why is that? Well, *where sin abounded, grace abounded much more!* God's desire was to pour out grace on His family; and

He knew the only way to do that was to give something which would cause the abundance of sin.

This leads to something else. If we are going to use the Old Testament law and commandments to determine sin, we need to be careful. If we call actions that were disallowed under the law "sin", then we make a sinner out of Christ. I know it is hard to swallow, but I will prove it. The first thing we have to understand is that, according to James 2:10, being guilty of any portion of the law makes you guilty of it all.

Secondly, according to the law the following things were *illegal*. (Note Jesus' actions alongside these laws):

- Touching a woman with her discharge – (Matt 9) the woman with a 12-year issue of blood touches Jesus. Granted, He did not touch her; but the touch is still there.
- Touching a leper – (Mark 1) Jesus heals the leper who asks if He is willing.
- Sabbath Work – (Luke 6) Jesus and His disciples pick grain on the Sabbath.

These are three simple examples. We cannot define sin by lawful or unlawful actions. Therefore, sin must be defined in a different manner. But how do we define it? Well, simply put *sin* is this: anything done trying to attain God's presence, appearance, or power – and all because of an indwelling identity crisis. Whenever we think our actions can make us worthy of fellowship with the Father that is *sin*. Whenever we think our actions can make us look more like God that is *sin*. Whenever we think our actions can somehow grant us the power of the Father, that action becomes *sin*. I know this changes some paradigms. It is meant to . . . God always intendeds for us to understand; we *are* just like Him! If we think for one minute God gave the law so rape, murder, homosexuality, child molestation, slavery, or any other thing that we call a despicable act might abound, we are wrong! God gave the law so the real meaning of sin might abound; so humanity would see that nothing they could do would ever allow them the appearance, power, or position of God (because that was His gift to mankind - our identity). The very reason Adam was not supposed to eat of the tree of knowledge was because eating of that tree would precipitate comparing himself to the God with whom he had already been in fellowship. And in that comparison, perceived separation would come.

God made the separation of sin and action for us in Hebrews 10:17 when He says *their sins and their lawless deeds I will remember no more*. God's action forever made the separation from what *sin* actually is, and what all the other stuff we label as sin is: lawless deeds. This makes a shipwreck of religion because if sin is now anything we do in order to be more like God in appearance, power or position, then most of our religious activity could be classified as sin. If we are worshiping, giving, attending, fasting, or even praying just to fulfill the old religious adage of "trying to be more like God", then we are walking in something that could be labeled as sin! Those things we have spent so much time trying to call sin, homosexuality, murder, rape, adultery, etc. are lawless deeds; and, we should stay away from them. But,

God's point was our *sins* and our *lawless deeds* would no more be remembered!

We have been that taught sin is "missing the mark" and although that is partially true, I do not believe it encompasses the internal disease that summarizes what sin really is. It is an infection of sorts - a sickness - in which we go through life doing anything to attain to our real identity, which has been given freely by the Father. The "mark" we are missing is the truth of who we really are and what we have been brought into.

Missing the mark of our inclusion into the life and fellowship of the Father, Son and Spirit causes all sorts of things in our lives, such as sickness, disease, emotional issues, refusal to fellowship, avoidance of others, and a myriad of other life issues which are all a result of an internal disease called sin. When we do not understand who we are, and what we have been brought into, then all sorts of rotten fruits begin to manifest. If we are really religious, it manifests as church attendance, tithing, fasting, intercessory prayer, shouting in tongues, etc. If we are anti-religious, it manifests as the avoidance of those things. Both outcomes are incorrect, because we miss the heart of the Father when we work on either side of that pendulum.

Okay, now back to our point from Romans. God gave the law so sin could abound. Now we know actions do not determine sin. We have to understand that the only *sin* of which man is capable is thinking he needs to *do* anything in order to be more like God, look more like God, or have fellowship with God.

Therefore, now sin must be an indwelling identity crisis. C. Baxter Kruger says it this way; sin is insisting Jesus must believe in us, rather than us believe in Him! What a powerful statement. We all face this crisis from time to time and dealing with that crisis determines our actions. When we understand who we are and what Jesus Christ has done for us, it gives birth to love, joy, peace, faith, worship, and salvation's fullness in our lives. When we do not have a grasp of who He made us to be, and what He did for us, it gives birth to fear, lack, sickness, disease, and even things like atheism, polytheism, and all sorts of false doctrines of *us*.

God wanted mankind to see the utter failure of thinking He was not near them and the lie of thinking they needed to do something to make Him love them more. There was no single thing that could ever have been done to increase God's love for humanity. He started this whole thing with perfect love for man, which remained perfect throughout history up to this point of consummation of which we are alluding.

If we look at Romans again, we begin to see where this path is leading us. Because of the offense of one, judgment came to all people. Then, through One Man's righteous act (the finishing of mankind's adoption by Christ) the free gift (salvation) came to ALL people. Religion will not like this. The religious will say only those who have held up their hands, prayed an "abra-ca-Jesus" prayer, or made some confession of faith are saved. Paul made it abundantly clear for us in this passage that because of the ONE act of righteousness, the free gift came to all people. God's gifts do not return to Him a failure. They always accomplish that which they are set out to accomplish. The Father, Son and Spirit had conspired from the beginning to save all humanity and bring them all into the family.

A GOSPEL OF RECONCILIATION

We briefly touched on the ministry of reconciliation once, but now I would like to visit it again.

> **2 Corinthians 5:18** - *Now all things are of God, who has reconciled us to Himself through Jesus Christ, and has given us the ministry of reconciliation.*

We must start reading with intent; either we have all been reconciled to God through Christ, or not. If so, then we need to live like it, and live like everyone else is too. If not, then we are all doomed no matter what we do. But, if He did, it is time we start to live, share, and teach like everyone with whom we come into contact is walking around with Christ in them. They need a wakeup call more than they need another message on hell, or the typical *"if you died tonight, where would you go"* speech. Look at what Paul says next, because it is amazing!

> **2 Corinthians 5:19** - *that is, that God was in Christ reconciling the world to Himself, not*

imputing their trespasses to them, and has committed to us the word of reconciliation.

God was in Christ, reconciling the world to Himself. What, the world? The whole world? And what else? NOT IMPUTING THEIR TRESPASSES!!! That statement bears repeating, because, if 2000 years ago God was not imputing their trespasses, what makes us think that He is doing it today? He has committed to us the word of reconciliation. And so many so-called grace preachers are terrified of the word reconciliation. Well, I am not. All people, ALL PEOPLE, have been reconciled to God - once, for all, forever.

2 Corinthians 5:20 - *Now then, we are ambassadors for Christ, as though God were pleading through us: we implore you on Christ's behalf, be reconciled to God.*

This might seem contradictory to what I just said, but we need to look at this verse more closely. The statement 'be reconciled to God' would be contradictory to Paul's statement that all people are reconciled, unless it is more along the lines of 'come home' - just like the prodigal son. Then we have the final verse in this chapter.

2 Corinthians 5:21 - *For He made Him who knew no sin [to be] sin for us, that we might become the righteousness of God in Him.*

There is no such thing as 'thrown away' righteousness; there is no giving this up. If anything we can do is able to eliminate or remove the gift of God, then we would have been able to save ourselves, as well. We all know we could never have done it. If we could have saved ourselves to begin with, God would not have needed to love us so much nor send His son to forever redeem all of humanity. He would not have needed to die as us, in our place, and raise us with Him.

Look at what Paul says in Romans:

Romans 6:7 - *for he who has died has been freed from sin.*

Paul again tells us that if we have died, we have been freed from sin. This chapter is used to abuse people and manipulate them into obedience to the professional behind the pulpit. But, the verses are full of Paul imploring us to realize we are not sinful beings anymore. We are not subject to the power of sin; we are not subject to the wages of sin. We are freed from sin, because if one died for all, then all died. Keep in mind Paul was dealing with a generation of people, who lived before and after the cross of Christ, people who were on both sides of the 'crucifixion fence'. This generation of people lived under the law, and under freedom. We have only ever known freedom. We have only ever known grace. Much with which we have been pummeled was teaching meant to show this generation of believers they were no longer subject to past sin.

Either Christ defeated the power of sin, or He did not. Either He did what He set out to do, or He did not. We have lived like He did not. We have gone through our lives struggling with what we have called sin, or rather, what our religious leaders have called sin. We have felt the condemnation of man, which we have been told is the conviction of the Holy Spirit, for things God never classified as sin.

No matter what we do, nothing can ever make us become *not* His children. We can be disobedient, treat each other wrongly, and do things to each other to cause damage, physical pain, or even death. We cannot cease to be His children.

So I can do What I Want?

No! We are taught that unless we acknowledge our sin, God will not forgive us; we are taught that unless we confess every despicable act to God, we cannot walk in love. We are taught that if there were not a teaching of our sin in the church, the only logical teaching would be to tell people they can just go do whatever they want. Not true. Remember the bible is much less a map to heaven or hell, and much more a manual for physical existence - a handbook of relationships.

When we really understand the love of Christ, and the love of the Father, we will stop treating each other so poorly.

Sadly enough, I have been more abused, neglected, and rejected during my time in the church than I ever was in the so-called secular world. Usually it is because of some 'sin' in my life someone had determined is the one sin beyond the grace, love and mercy of God. Yep, that is the one for which Jesus did not die. *That one right there.* Do we listen to ourselves? Do we really hear what we live?

We tell people God loves them just as they are; then, the second they get in the door, we begin trying to change them. The only thing that can ever change us or make us stop the actions which cause so much pain, is the love and grace of God. Until we allow people to experience God's love in their own way and on their own time, all we are doing is heaping on more rules and regulations. Paul told us that the strength of sin is the law. The law which we give people is the very reason they continue in whatever action we have determined to be wrong.

I will add here that transgression against one another is something we need to (daily) repent of. When I hurt you, I have a responsibility to repent for that hurt. James tells us to confess our sins one to another that we can be made whole. From the standpoint of God (theologically) Jesus has forever answered the issue of sin. However, from the standpoint of our human relationships (ontologically) we have a responsibility to not only behave in a manner fitting the gospel – to love one another – but also to repent when we find ourselves in positions of hurt and abuse toward one another. Jesus is all about our love for one another, and that is the heart of the message. We can refrain from calling that activity *sin* if we like, but we are playing a semantic game. I cannot *sin* against God because, vertically speaking, the issue is no longer an issue. I can however, *sin* against you through abusive attitudes and applications.

More people need to get this message. How about showing acceptance to the guy with crooked teeth who stinks to high heaven? How about showing a little grace to the woman caught in adultery? We are so busy throwing her out of the office and demanding her resignation that we actually forget that she needs grace and love. Jesus would have restored her identity and given her love. He did back then, and He still does today.

REPENTANCE

The lifeblood of the western church has been calling sinners to repentance. We have made it a prerequisite for knowing Christ that people repent from their sins, and repent from their wicked thoughts. We preach repentance daily in our pulpits, pounding them while announcing one sin over another. What if we have been wrong? What if repentance is not so much about turning from sin as it is turning to God? What if God repented (gasp), would that change our approach?

Exodus 32:14 (KJV) - *And the LORD repented of the evil which he thought to do unto his people.*

So if we are going to label repentance as turning from sin, then we have just labeled the creator as being subject to sin. He is not, but we do not make these associations in our mind as we preach.

Repentance is a simple change of mind. It means to turn and go the other direction. There is no sin found in the word, and no admission of wrong done. The Lord simply changed His mind in this passage and decided to go a different route. Is God capable of doing whatever He wants? Yes. And yet, He decided to go a different way with the people.

This is what we are to call people to do, to change their minds about the Father. We ought to be apologizing to the world for the way Christians have treated them, for our judgment and wrath, for our disgust at their lives. We ought to repent. If the world can simply change their mind about the Father, His love, and the sacrifice of Christ, then actions will follow suit. We get so caught up in trying to impose morality on people that we forget it is all about their identity. Morality follows identity, and starting with the end takes us right back to what I call "destinational" Christianity (we will talk more about this concept later).

CHAPTER 8
CONTEXTUAL MATH

"The formulation of the problem is often more essential than its solution"
Albert Einstein

To PROPERLY BEGIN to define the Word and to rightly divide it, we need to take a contextual approach in our reading. We learned earlier that the principle behind this idea of contextual math is this: if x=something and y=something, then x + y=something. Using this logic, we can really begin to dig deeper into the scriptures to see things we have either never seen, or have begun to ignore due to religious fear, ignorance, or just plain rebellion. Not rebellion to God necessarily, but rebellion to what we fear we may see if we dig deeper. For some, "deeper" has become a word to fear.

I AND MY FATHER ARE ONE

For the first lesson in our contextual math class, we are going to take a look at the statement of Christ in John 10:30 that says *I and my Father are one* (KJV). This is our 'x=' portion of the first equation. X = Jesus and the Father are One. Next, we have Christ's statement in John 5:19 that says *the Son can do nothing of Himself, but what He sees the Father do; for whatever He does, the Son also does in like manner* . Here is our 'y=' part of the equation. Y=Jesus does what the Father does. So our equation thus far is shaping up like this: X=(Jesus and Father are one) and Y=(Jesus and Father do the same thing). So if Jesus and the Father are one, and everything Jesus does is what the Father would do, then everything Jesus did is what the Father would have done. I know this may sound unnecessarily simple, but stick with me, because it is something we have lost in this day and age. Taking our x and y into account, we need to read the acts of Christ in a new light that, if He did it, it is what the Father would have done in that particular situation.

> John 8:10-11 - *When Jesus had raised Himself up and saw no one but the woman, He said to her, "Woman, where are those accusers of yours? Has no one condemned you?" She said, "No one, Lord." And Jesus said to her, "Neither do I condemn you; go and sin no more."*

Our equation leads us to this conclusion: that if Jesus did not condemn this woman, then the Father did not condemn her either. The one who claimed to be one with the Father in two verses, with just one thought, not only releases this woman from condemnation, but also restores her identity. The adultery in which she was caught had become her identity; or in other words, to the Jewish leader, she was now *an adulteress*. No longer was she a woman, but now something lower than a mere woman; she was an adulteress. This is much like the church today. We label people as homosexuals, adulterers, murderers, gossips, backstabbers, or whatever label we have chosen to be our particular hot button. We change their identity to whatever *sin* in which they happen to be caught, instead of who they really are. In one fell swoop, the one who claimed to do only as He saw the Father do, releases this woman from certain death, restores her identity as a woman, and sends her on her way. Religion would have us focus on *go and sin no more*, without ever addressing the identity issue that had caused the problem in the first place. Christ will *always* deal with our identity first. When our identity is healed and restored, we will have the ability to walk away from whatever has trapped us. When will we start to act like Jesus and restore the identity of those stuck in the mire? Jesus spoke *daughter* and *woman* and *son* and *man*, never once speaking their sin as who they were.

AS HE IS...

For the second lesson, I want to look at another statement of whose reality and power we fail to grasp. John said in 1 John 4:17 that *Love has been perfected among us in this: that we may have boldness in the day of judgment; because **as He is**, so are we in this world.* This is a powerful statement on its own. It is an 'x' that does not really need a 'y' for the equation to work, but we should press on. We are going to borrow the 'x' from the previous equation and make it our 'y' for this one. *I and my Father are one.* So if x=(as He is, so are we) and y=(He and the Father are one) then we and the Father are one. This is astounding! We have yet to grasp our oneness with the Father.

I can hear the struggle in your mind, *but I do understand my oneness with the Father.* Let me make this clear. If we (we includes me) are struggling with our health, our prosperity, our mental ability, our emotional state, depression, anger, fear or lack, we are not experiencing what the Father Himself is experiencing; then, we do not grasp our oneness. This is not an accusation - it is freedom! If we can grasp that we are not fully aware of what the Father provided, then we can begin to pray in a way that will accomplish something in our lives. Instead of asking for money, joy, peace, love or health, all we need is a prayer of *Father, help me understand my oneness with You.* In the oneness which Christ provided there is everything we can ever need for this life and the next!

This same equation applies across the board for everything we read about the person of Jesus Christ. Everything He is, we are. Everything He has, we have. And, everywhere He is, we are.

Hebrews 8:1 - *Now this is the main point of the things we are saying: We have such a High Priest, who is seated at the right hand of the throne of the Majesty in the heavens.*

If we are as Him, then we are also seated at the right hand of the throne of the Majesty. This has many marvelous implications. Is there sickness at the right hand of the throne? Is there poverty? Is there lack? Is there sin? Is there struggle? No! There is only freedom at the right hand of the Father, and it is time for the world to awaken and receive their birthright – this freedom.

THE SUM OF IT ALL

The equation of salvation to many believers works something like this. Jesus + my works = salvation. Somewhere along the line, we have adopted the belief that Jesus needs our help for our complete salvation. This is a fatal flaw; because the moment we add ourselves to the equation, we add frail humanity. Jesus did what He did without our help, without our input, and without our involvement. He does not need us to finish the already finished work! He did not hang on the cross and say "it will be finished if…" or "it is a good start"!

To others, it works something like this. Jesus + my faith = salvation. Again, there is a problem with this equation. We have just added to the person of Christ with something that we think carries any importance or power, our faith. What did Paul say? *The life I now live, I live in the faith OF the Son of God.* If it is Christ's faith we now live in, then what leads us to believe that it is our faith that adds to our salvation? It does not!

The most poisonous version of this equation relates like this: my faith + my works = salvation. Hopefully, since you are reading this book, this does not apply to you. What a failing equation this is! There is no power or success in this equation. There is no victory at all!

So what is the real equation of salvation? Jesus' Work + Jesus' Faith = Salvation. Plain and simple, if it is not all Him, it is not Him at all! We have to understand that we could never have done this. The Father knew this; therefore, He once and for all provided all things for all people through the one sacrifice of His Son. We have nothing to bring to the table of salvation, save one thing. Belief. Please do not make the mistake of creating an inseparable synonym out of belief and faith. These are two separate things. Faith is *of* Christ. Belief is *of* us. We place our belief, frail and imperfect as it may be, in the finished work of Christ; and this because, He has done His priestly job of presenting us to the Father as holy, blameless, and above reproach.

CHAPTER 9
ALL YOU NEED IS LOVE

"Nothing you can make that cannot be made, No one you can save that cannot be saved, Nothing you can do but you can learn how to be you in time. It's easy – All you need is love"
The Beatles

I F THERE IS ONE THING the Beatles got right, it is that love is all we need. Not the love of man, however, but the love of the One Who *is* love. To be loved by the perfect image of love can heal the broken hearted, repair the wounded, restore the lost, and revive the dead. However, in order to have an image of the great love with which He loves us, we must look at a few things, and again, use our contextual math to form a better image of Father, Papa, Daddy, and Abba.

> 1 John 4:7-8 - *Beloved, let us love one another, for love is of God; and everyone who loves is born of God and knows God. He who does not love does not know God, for God is love.*

God is love. We say it, put it on bumper stickers, write it on t-shirts, and proclaim it to the world with church advertising. However, people usually discover that we proclaim God is love with our mouths, and then preach His judgment from our pulpits. We put a facade of *hospital* on our church buildings while the inside is nothing short of a courtroom full of judges and juries.

We have lost sight of what love really is; and so, in like manner, who God is. We need to recapture the vision of love and recapture the vision of *GOD* as Father.

> 1 Corinthians 13:4-8a - *Love suffers long and is kind; love does not envy; love does not parade itself, is not puffed up, does not behave rudely, does not seek its own, is not provoked, thinks no evil; does not rejoice in iniquity, but rejoices in the truth; bears all things, believes all things, hopes all things, endures all things. Love never fails.*

We have had this passage preached to us from every angle. It has been used to show what the marriage covenant should look like, what ministry should look like, and what we should be doing in our daily lives. There are good points to take from this but we have missed the major point because we do not understand contextual math.

If God is love, and we transpose that over onto this passage, we can see something about the character of our Father that has largely been overlooked. *God suffers long and is kind; God does not envy; God does not parade Himself, is not puffed up, does not behave rudely, does not seek His own, is not provoked, thinks no evil; does not rejoice in iniquity, but rejoices in the truth; bears all things, believes all things, hopes all things, endures all things. God never fails.*

Does this sound like the Father in whom we believe? Or does it sound like a pipe dream that has no place inside our religion? We have to begin to read the letters of Paul, Peter, James and the others with some real context. Context does not just grab the verses in the chapters around it; it takes into account the whole picture. If the whole picture of our Father is He is love, then it stands to reason that every passage that deals with the subject of love also deals with the Father.

This does something to our *faith* as well. It begins forming a better view of what we are really talking about.

1 Corinthians 13:13 - *And now abide faith, hope, love, these three; but the greatest of these is love.*

Read that verse again. The *greatest* of these is love? That alone should place some need to rethink on those who would preach *your* faith, *your* works, and *your* commitment.

Faith and hope abide, but both are lesser than love; both are lesser than God. God's love for us surpasses our so-called faith. It exceeds the hope that those under the Old Covenant had in looking forward to their Savior. It goes beyond everything we can throw at it. If the greatest of all things is love (God), then why do we place such high value on our faith? We should not! It is the faith *of* Christ in which we live, the only perfect faith that ever has been, or ever could be.

SEPARATION ANXIETY

This world is plagued with separation anxiety largely due to the teachings of the church. We have been taught that our sin separates us from the Father; that He cannot abide sin, tolerate our pride, failings, or lack of faith. We have an image of the Father as a standoffish, feeble old man who does not want involvement with us, but holds us at bay so He does not have to be in direct contact with us. We forget that in the beginning God walked out of the garden with Adam, forever dispelling the lie that He cannot abide sin.

If sin could or does separate us from the Father, and we cannot be in His presence with sin in our lives, then we need to understand one thing: Jesus Christ was both a miserable failure, and was not one with the Father as He said. For Christ to take all of our sin on Himself at the crucifixion, while still being one with the Father, He *had* to be able to abide sin! This is a big statement I know; but we need to grasp this. If God could not abide sin, then Christ could not have; and His sacrifice was in vain. Not so! God *can* abide sin, and He still does! He does not condone our behaviors; He wants us to walk out of them in freedom and peace. However, when we teach this message that the Father cannot abide sin and separates us from Him, then what we are saying is in direct contradiction to the Father's own words in Deuteronomy 31:6, 8 and Joshua 1:5 that says *I will NEVER leave you nor forsake you!*

Never leave?

Even when we sin?

Never leave.

Even when we fail?

Never leave.

Even when we do not believe?

Never leave.

Even when we do not successfully measure up?

Never leave.

Even when we do not make a profession of faith?

Never leave!

This is a powerful truth!

> **Romans 8:38-39** - *For I am persuaded that neither death nor life, nor angels nor principalities nor powers, nor things present nor things to come, nor height nor depth, nor any other created thing, shall be able to separate us from the love of God which is in Christ Jesus our Lord.*

Our discussion needs to lead us to this truth: nothing can separate us from the love of God. If we truly understand and believe what we have already mentioned, that God *is* love, then we need to grasp something here. If God is love and nothing can separate us, then nothing can separate us from God. I know some religious alarms just went off in all your heads screaming words you want to say to me; but let me clarify. To be separate from the love of the Father is to be separate from the Father Himself. To the Roman church Paul wrote: nothing, not death nor life, not angels nor demons, not ANY created thing (of which the devil and humanity are a part) can separate us from God's love.

The lie in the garden was a lie of separation. The serpent ministered separation to the mind of Eve as she whispered to herself "you can be like God" creating a thought in her mind of separation from her Father. This lie is what we continue to converse with today and has borne all sorts of problems. Psychology has begun to prove something fairly amazing, which if applied to our current Christology, can show us why we are in the state we are in today. That proof is this (see diagram): All wrath (anger) stems from fear. All fear stems from insecurity, and all insecurity stems from separation anxiety at some point in life. It may have been as a child when they cannot remember, but the underlying problem is always separation! This is astonishing is it not? The world is proving what the gospel has always shown; that if we will minister reconciliation, everything will change!

caleb miller

1 John 4:16 - And we have known and believed the love that God has for us. God is love, and he who abides in love abides in God, and God in him.

It is not enough to just *know* that God loves us; we need to *believe* it. This is not a statement of faith, but of belief. Our belief is an opening, the smallest crack in the door of our hearts. And as we open the door, the Father is standing, waiting for the chance to simply slide His foot in the door, and blow it open, bursting through our darkness with love. This is why it is so important to bring a message of love to the world. There are unbelievers all over this earth who have yet to open their eyes to the rescue God has provided and the love with which it was brought. Love opens their eyes, and pierces the darkness. Love heals the wounds and restores the broken. Love breaks the hardest heart, and comforts the softest. Love is all you need.

CHAPTER 10

KEEPING THE MAIN THING THE MAIN THING

"Beware lest you lose the substance by grasping at the shadow."
Aesop

THERE IS A NECESSITY in the body of Christ today to recover something I feel has largely been lost in all of our theological debates, instruction in righteousness, and even our understanding of grace. We have lost focus of one simple fact, one simple statement by John the disciple of Jesus, which is: *"in the beginning was the word, and the word was with God, and the word was God"*. In order to refocus our belief, our identity and even our religion, we need to recapture this truth. Before moving on with the principle that this book is founded upon, we need to address this refocusing that ought to happen.

Our bible is not written as a novel, with proper character development and back-story. Also, it is not written as a documentary with correct chronological placement of all events in the structure and makeup of the books. If it were, I am convinced we would open up the word to *"in the beginning was the word...."* and then progress on to *"and in the beginning, God created the heavens and the earth..."*. We must realize that the Father, Son and Holy Spirit were together from before there was time and will be together for all eternity.

This is paramount to all discussions of faith, worship, offerings, communion, prayer, and any other life pursuits. We treat our bible as though it were broken into three sections: (see fig.. 1)

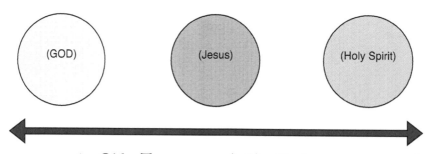

1. Old Testament (left) God - angry and unwilling to fellowship with man.
2. The Gospels (middle) Jesus - appeasing an angry and judgmental God.

3. New Testament (right) Holy Spirit - sent to make us weird, to exalt ourselves because of our Gift and cause a ruckus among the body of Christ.

We need to refocus a bit on the truth of the word. We do not have a separatist Father, a God who does not fellowship with His counterparts, and acts on His own. We have a Father who, during the fall, removed us from the garden for our own protection, lest we combine our newfound knowledge of good and evil (separation) with eternal life. With our understanding that *in the beginning was the word...*, He did not stand behind watching us from afar but came out with us to live in fellowship, as did the person of Jesus Christ and the Holy Spirit with whom He shares all things.

Now we must apply this understanding to every discussion of the Old Testament. It is no longer a book about a God whose wrath needed to be appeased, or whose judgment needed fulfillment. But it is a collection of stories of mankind's dispersion around the earth, either hiding from, or running to the presence of "GOD" (not running to *Father* as He intended, but rather changing Father and Friend into King and God).

The refocus needs to take place on the statements of Jesus - *I and my Father are one...* (John 10:30), and of Paul - *that is, that God was in Christ reconciling the world to Himself, not imputing their trespasses to them* (2 Corinthians 5:19). This changes our three-part focus of the word into something different. It says if God was in Christ and Jesus and His father are one, the written word can now be broken down into these three parts: (see fig. 2)

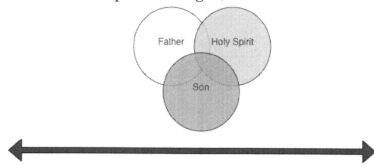

1.   Old Testament Father, Son, and Holy Spirit - Together, fellowshipping with humanity, longing for humankind to understand their right standing and fellowship.

2.   The Gospels Father, Son, and Holy Spirit - Working together, reconciling all people unto the Father, with the Son acting as mediator, the Spirit leading Him, and the Father showing Him what to do and say (*I only do as I see my Father do...*)

3.   New Testament Father, Son, and Holy Spirit - together with the spirit guiding us into all truth, showing us the power and communion of the Father and Son.

This is the base upon which our foundation must come. We can never remove one person of the Trinity from our theology, or, by necessity, we remove all three. If the three exist in such close fellowship that it can only be called *mutual indwelling*, then the removal of one (whether in our thinking or deeds) necessitates the removal of all three. I want to look first at what Jesus says immediately after being raised from the dead.

Matthew 28:19 - *"Go therefore and make disciples of all the nations, baptizing them in the name of the Father and of the Son and of the Holy Spirit"*

Jesus gives His final instruction before heading back home. Note first of all that He is not commanding that we *Go therefore and make converts of everyone we meet.* Why? Because Jesus took care of the conversion for us. He bore all mankind in Himself upon the cross and He had total faith in His finished work. What He is saying is this: go and *teach* all people. This word teach means something as a time consuming, line upon line type of teaching. It is why I will not pursue a *"seeker-sensitive"* methodology in my ministry; and why the ministry of the teacher is so important in the body of Christ. Now, moving on to what we are to do *after* teaching. Baptizing them. Jesus is instructing us to make others aware of their cleanliness *in* the name of the Father AND of the Son AND of the Holy Spirit. You see, only the union of the three persons of the Trinity affects true cleanliness of spirit. The Father knew this and He took care of it for us. He sent His Son to make us clean; and now, the Son is seated with the Father in perfect unity, fully at rest that He accomplished what He was sent to accomplish.

The Holy Spirit is a misused, misunderstood, and misapplied personality of the Trinity. We do not fully grasp the importance and purpose of His presence with us. We see something special in the first appearances of the Holy Spirit in the New Testament:

> Matthew 3:16-17 - *When He had been baptized, Jesus came up immediately from the water; and behold, the heavens were opened to Him, and He saw the Spirit of God descending like a dove and alighting upon Him. And suddenly a voice [came] from heaven, saying, "This is My beloved Son, in whom I am well pleased."*

Occurrence #1 of the Holy Spirit's presence in the New Testament, and notice something.

- It is not to "give a word"
- It is not to "speak in tongues"
- It is not to "direct the service"

What He appeared for, or rather because of, was the union of Father and Son. The Holy Spirit is like stage lighting. His appearance happens because the Father met the Son in a real way, and whenever that happens, the light of the Spirit comes to show light on that union. This is what happens upon every reunion of Father and Son today. As we begin to awaken people to their union with the Father, the Holy Spirit flings the door open, shines the light on that reunion, and our family has become so much fuller!

First and foremost, the Spirit is here to shed light on the union of Father and Son. He is here to direct us back to the communion they share.

John 14:26 - *"But the Helper, the Holy Spirit, whom the Father will send in My name, He will teach you all things, and bring to your remembrance all things that I said to you.*

Occurrence #2 - The Spirit is here to teach us all things and bring to remembrance the words of Christ. I know you are reading this book hoping I will teach you something; but it is the Holy Spirit's job to teach you, not mine. I am simply writing my thoughts and personal revelations down, in hopes that the Holy Spirit will ignite something inside of you.

Acts 2:4 - *And they were all filled with the Holy Spirit and began to speak with other tongues, as the Spirit gave them utterance.*

Occurrence #3 – This is the first manifestation of the Spirit that results in a *gift* being used. Notice it is not a gift to uplift a man, or make him into something Jesus Himself has become in our stead (prophet, priest, etc.) Far too often the gifts of the Spirit are nothing of the Spirit at all, but rather a man using his place to exalt himself. What happened in Acts as a result of the gift of the Spirit? THOUSANDS were brought to an understanding of Jesus Christ as their propitiation. He has the final word.

Much of this may seem basic and elementary; however, what we must do is start here. We need to set our focus back on the fact that the three persons of the Godhead are in intimate fellowship, eternally, and powerfully. This is the starting place of all human history and where we ourselves must begin. To move forward in our doctrinal discourse, theological studies, and even our ministry lives, we must recapture this vision of the Godhead. This book could begin here, with everything preceding this being a foreword of sorts.

A NOTE ON THE BAPTISM OF CHRIST

The baptism of Jesus was a peculiar event. The Messiah, coming to the messenger for immersion? It seems backwards. What we must understand about the baptism of Jesus is this; John, like many of his contemporaries, expected a Messiah who would rule with governmental power and authority, the kind that overthrows kings and kingdoms. Jesus certainly did this, but not in the manner expected. Jesus was, just as the Father is, non-violent. His commitment to peace extended to the Roman guard that came to arrest Him (Peter, put away your sword), to the guards tearing Him to shreds on the whipping post, and then to the cross, where His refusal to "call down the angels" showed His final heart towards violence. I believe that Jesus' peaceful submission to John showed those who were around the event that their vision of the Messiah was skewed. Jesus willingly and peacefully allowed the messenger to baptize Him, and that initial act of submission and peace rendered new light to the kind of Messiah He was to be.

CHAPTER 11

FINE TUNING
THE LENSES

"He set it all out before us in Christ, a long-range plan in which
everything would be brought together and summed up in him"
Ephesians 1:10 (MESSAGE)

OW THAT WE HAVE RESET our lenses and can see where the
foundation of our faith, religious pursuit, etc. must
come from, we should begin to fine tune those lenses a
bit. We understand the Father, Son, and Holy Spirit are,
always have been and always will be inseparable (one will not
work without the other); they do not operate independently,
but as one (anything one does is what the other two would
do as well). We can see the Godhead as a "blessed Trinity" as

Hays said in his hymn *Holy, Holy, Holy*. If we can lay hold of this truth, it will change our lives when we combine it with the following.

The Apostle Paul was the guy. He was God's *Tony Soprano*, the head honcho of the grace message. Two things I want to quickly say about Paul before going further into this.

1.   Paul spent somewhere between 3 and 7 years (I have even heard reference to something like 14 years!) in the desert alone with Christ . . . not conferring with flesh and blood, not discussing his doctrine with theologians, not worrying himself with growing a church, not concerned with the religious leadership. Just focusing on Jesus and what He had to say. Paul certainly had a Jesus-centered theology, above all else.

2.   Paul is the one who said *For now we know in part* (1 Corinthians 13:9). The number one phraseology in all of Paul's letters is *With Him*, and *In Him* (and variations of those, such as through him, through whom, etc.)

This says a couple things to me:

First, in all of our study, theology degrees, doctorates, bible college attendance records, and Sunday school classes, we will simply never know the fullness of what was given. The best way we can describe it, pales in comparison with the true glory the Father offers. We will never have a 100% picture of His goodness, how much He did for us and loves us - until we are with Him. Second, if the man who for years spoke personally with Christ, *alone* in the desert, says something over and over again, we need to take note, stand up, pay attention and give preference to it! So what is the truth we need to grasp here?

Once again, we have to look at our view of the Father, Son, and Holy Spirit to find out how to approach this. Religion thinks we are separate from the Father because of our sin, our shortfall, or our beliefs.

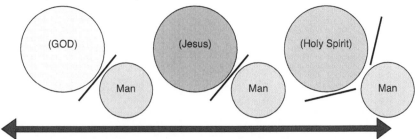

1. Old Testament (left) God - angry and unwilling to fellowship with man - holding man at bay, lest humanity's badness rub off on God's goodness. Note the "wall of separation" firmly between mankind and the Father.

2. The Gospels (middle) Jesus - appeasing an angry and judgmental God - still holding man out, commanding that we be perfect just as our Father is perfect. The wall of separation is still firmly in place, this time with the Son holding us at bay.

3. New Testament (right) Holy Spirit - here to make us weird, to exalt ourselves because of our Gift, and here to cause a ruckus among the body of Christ. He allows us in, but only upon the confession of our guilt and 'repentance' from our sin. We can squeeze through the narrow opening, but only if we fit the mold religion has given us.

These misconceptions are destructive, deadly and the reason for all manner of religion on earth today. If we had been living and teaching what Paul taught for the last 2000 years, the world would know and accept what we do!

First we ought to deal with this horrid vision of the unapproachable GOD in the Old Testament.

> **Leviticus 26:9-13** - *For I will look on you favorably and make you fruitful, multiply you and confirm My covenant with you. You shall eat the old harvest, and clear out the old because of the new. I will set My tabernacle among you, and My soul shall not abhor you. I will walk among you and be your God, and you shall be My people. I am the Lord your God, who brought you out of the land of Egypt, that you should not be their slaves; I have broken the bands of your yoke and made you walk upright.*

The Father speaks to His children with acceptance, love, and inclusion. He shares with them that His heart, the very center of His being is to walk among them and to look favorably upon them!

> **Ezekiel 37:26-28** - *Moreover I will make a covenant of peace with them, and it shall be an everlasting covenant with them; I will establish them and multiply them, and I will set My sanctuary in their midst forevermore. My*

tabernacle also shall be with them; indeed I will be their God, and they shall be My people. The nations also will know that I, the Lord, sanctify Israel, when My sanctuary is in their midst forevermore.

Again, the Father is saying His covenant is an everlasting covenant of peace, one of walking and being one with them! We have the Father who constantly approaches us. His desire was always to walk with us in the cool of the day like He did with Adam in the garden. His purpose and plan was to have a family to inhabit the earth; and He would be here with us! So often we focus on *one day when we get to heaven*, we forget that this earth was created for us, as our home where Father and Sons would commune forever in perfect communion! We must (and this is of utmost importance) understand that the Father was not a vengeful, rageaholic in the Old Testament and a peacenick in the new. He is the One of whom we hear "I am the Lord, I do not change". Romans 5 tells us that the law was given that the offense should abound, and where sin abounded, grace did much more. This means that there was grace, even under the law, for the Old Testament folks. This is contrary to what we have been taught concerning grace and law, but we must understand that grace and law are not antonyms. They have very little to do with one another. The law was basic instructions for life, and nearly all the laws dealt with showing man what trying to be "like" God looked like. The opposite of the law is freedom. Jesus delivered the perfect law of liberty to us, that is for certain, but to say there was no grace for the Old Testament guys and gals is to say that the Father is a dispensational GOD, bound by covenant rather than His unfailing love.

Now I want to turn our focus to the so-called unapproachable Christ in the Gospels.

> **Matthew 9:20-22** - *And suddenly, a woman who had a flow of blood for twelve years came from behind and touched the hem of His garment. For she said to herself, "If only I may touch His garment, I shall be made well." But Jesus turned around, and when He saw her He said, "Be of good cheer, daughter; your faith has made you well." And the woman was made well from that hour.*

This woman is under the impression Christ is trying to hold her at bay; that He is not here to minister to her, but to the masses. And how does Jesus meet this thought? *Be of good cheer Daughter.* He not only restores her joy, but also her identity. His calling her daughter immediately washes away the years of rejection by her peers because of her issue. This is a small town, and we all know how things go down in a small town!

> **John 4:9-19** - *Then the woman of Samaria said to Him, "How is it that You, being a Jew, ask a drink from me, a Samaritan woman?" For Jews have no dealings with Samaritans. Jesus answered and said*

to her, "If you knew the gift of God, and who it is who says to you, 'Give Me a drink,' you would have asked Him, and He would have given you living water." The woman said to Him, "Sir, You have nothing to draw with, and the well is deep. Where then do You get that living water? Are You greater than our father Jacob, who gave us the well, and drank from it himself, as well as his sons and his livestock?" Jesus answered and said to her, "Whoever drinks of this water will thirst again, but whoever drinks of the water that I shall give him will never thirst. But the water that I shall give him will become in him a fountain of water springing up into everlasting life." The woman said to Him, "Sir, give me this water, that I may not thirst, nor come here to draw." Jesus said to her, "Go, call your husband, and come here." The woman answered and said, "I have no husband." Jesus said to her, "You have well said, 'I have no husband,' for you have had five husbands, and the one whom you now have is not your husband; in that you spoke truly." The woman said to Him, "Sir, I perceive that You are a prophet.

This is probably my favorite story in the entire bible. We have a woman who is rejected by society, ostracized by her peers. She is a Samaritan, a second-class race, a woman, a second-class citizen, and a bit of a loose one at that, making her the lowest of the low. There was no lower person than her; because at least the prostitutes were paid for what they did. This woman was worse than a prostitute in the eyes of religious and political leaders because she did what she did for free. Our Savior, whom we view as holding man at bay, goes out of His way to reach this *lowest class* citizen. Her identity is healed and restored so much that she leaves shame at the well and runs into town shouting "I met a man!" Can you imagine what must have happened in this woman's heart to make her not think twice about proclaiming this fact to the multitude of her accusers? Can we picture the healing that took place to render her utterly and completely unashamed in the face of persecution and religious inquisition?

Now I want to talk about the Holy Spirit.

The Holy Spirit has a bad rap. He has been accused of convicting us of sin, constantly telling us how bad we are, how badly we need to repent and how covered in sin and shame we are.

John 16:13 – *However, when He, the Spirit of truth, has come, He will guide you into all truth; for He will not speak on His own authority, but whatever He hears He will speak; and He will tell you things to come.*

In this verse we see the primary function of the Spirit in our lives, to guide us into all truth and tell us things to come! We should go on before we go deeper.

Romans 8:15 - *For you did not receive the spirit of bondage again to fear, but you received the Spirit of adoption by whom we cry out, "Abba, Father."*

This is starting to shape up nicely, because we are beginning to see something about the Holy Spirit:

1. The Spirit is not just here to make us squirm around on the floor and shout in tongues (please note that I am not debating the validity of the experience of the Spirit, rather showing the primary function).

2. The Spirit is totally misunderstood!

The Holy Spirit is not the Spirit of bondage, holding us at bay, as though we were just lowly worms who have no right to be in the presence of the Father. He is the Spirit of Adoption, including all people inside the very life and communion of the Father, Son, and Holy Spirit! So, we need to understand there is something much deeper going on here. Earlier, I made reference to a truth that Paul taught more than any other truth. It is the truth of *us* with *Him*. This truth guided all of Paul's teaching, infiltrated every letter he wrote, every message he taught, and all the doctrine he set forth.

Ephesians 1:9 - *having made known to us the mystery of His will, according to His good pleasure which He purposed in Himself*

This is the NKJV. It says something I do not think is properly grasped. We should look at a few different versions to really get a broader picture of what is being offered.

Phillips - For God had allowed us to know the secret of his plan, and it is this:
Message - letting us in on the plans he took such delight in making.
New Living Translation - God has now revealed to us his mysterious plan regarding Christ, a plan to fulfill his own good pleasure.

These versions give a little more weight to this statement. There is something huge being said here. This is Paul, the guy who spent all this time alone with the Son, saying *the secret of God's plan, letting us in on the plans* and *revealed to us His mysterious plan regarding Christ, a plan to fulfill His own good pleasure.* To me, this is another area where we need to stand up and take note of what Paul is about to say. It is the greatest prelude to what I believe is the greatest truth in the word of God. If we could categorize our bible, this would be the pinnacle of our faith, the very *secret* of God's plan in sending His son!
And what is that secret?

Ephesians 1:10-12 [Message] - *He set it all out before us in Christ, a long-range plan in which everything would be brought together and summed up in him, everything in deepest heaven, everything on planet earth. It's in Christ that we find out who we are and what we are living for. Long before we first heard of Christ and got our hopes up, he had his eye on us, had designs on us for glorious living, part of the overall purpose he is working out in everything and everyone.*

V 10 [AMP] - *[He planned] for the maturity of the times and the climax of the ages to unify all things and head them up and consummate them in Christ, [both] things in heaven and things on the earth.*

V 10 [Phillips] - *he purposes in his sovereign will that all human history shall be consummated in Christ, that everything that exists in Heaven or earth shall find its perfection and fulfillment in him.*

I purposely went through these versions in order. We need to understand the *what, when* and *who*. You see, the Father did something in Christ we fail to grasp, because we are told wrongly that our adoption occurs only at the moment of belief. The Message Translation said here this was a long-range plan - it was the Father's master plan! He had what business schools call a 5/10/25 year plan, just a little longer! From the foundations of the world Jesus was foreordained to bring us in.

The What - The plan was that everything would be brought together and summed up in Him, in the deepest heaven and on planet earth!

The When - He planned for the maturity of the times and climax of the ages to unify all things! The climax is the high point - the point where Christ was lifted up on the cross is the highest point in human history!

The Who - I love the Phillips translation. *All Human History* - this means, all past, present and future humanity! Jesus did it all, for all, once and for all!

This is the truth as Paul knew it. It is the truth as we should know it. Our view now ought to be *With Him!*

Man is now in the very center of the Trinity, in intimate fellowship with the Father, through the Spirit, via the Son. We have access to the throne of grace because of the finished work, and this access is not granted by our good works, our belief, or our confession, it is granted by the Holy Spirit as He points us back to Christ.

A NOTE ON THREES

There is much significance given to the number three in the word of God. While I do not necessarily hold to all of the truths of digging around the "numberings" in the bible, I do see something in the value of the Trinity and the fact that there are three persons involved here. As I said before, the bible never uses the word Trinity; but the concept is clearly outlined in the word. Trinity is a human word, much like love. God is a concept God who outlines what our words mean. This means the Father, not man, defines love, though it is our English word that we use. Trinity is another word like that. It is an English word the Father defines as Father,

Son, and Holy Spirit. We have these three members of the Godhead, dwelling in unity and fellowship. Now also, we must understand that man is a three-part being. We are spirit, soul, and body. Our spirit is the eternal portion of our being, the part that has always been, and always will be. The Father spoke to the prophet Jeremiah in Chapter 1 and verse 5.

Jeremiah 1:5 - *"Before I formed you in the womb I knew you; Before you were born I sanctified you; I ordained you a prophet to the nations"*

Before Jeremiah was formed of flesh, the Father knew Him. This is evident also in the Garden of Eden when the Lord creates man in His image, male and female, a full chapter before He gives them their flesh garments.

The soul has been (rightly) defined as our mind, will and emotions. We know what the flesh is; in fact, we see it every day in our mirror. What we need to understand is that if we are to view the Godhead as a Trinity, a three-part Godhead into which we have been invited to fellowship, we can begin to superimpose our own existence onto the existence of the Trinity.

Spirit – The Father (John 4:24a – *God is spirit...*)

Soul – The Holy Spirit (Galatians 5:22-23 - *But the fruit of the Spirit is love, joy, peace, longsuffering, kindness, goodness, faithfulness, gentleness, self-control. Against such there is no law.*)

Body – The Son (Ephesians 5:30 - *For we are members of His body, of His flesh and of His bones.*)

We can overlay our own lives on the fellowship of the Trinity. The Father is spirit, as are we, in His image. The Holy Spirit's fruit is all the things that dictate our mind, will, and emotions. (An interesting side note is that the word *fruit* is singular, not plural. The fruit of the Spirit is all the mentioned things. It is not the fruit of the Spirit plus us; it is the Spirit alone who produces the fruit). The Son is a flesh and blood human, seated at the right hand of the Father, who lives to make intercession for us. We were not saved in part; and now it is up to us to redeem the other part. We were and are wholly saved!

In this same light, we can take the *jobs* of Jesus Christ and overlay again, prophet, priest, and king. We have a kingly Father who is the Lord, a prophet who is the Holy Spirit who reveals all things, and a great high priest who is the man Jesus Christ. The fellowship that the Trinity shares is so closely united that they have the unique ability to act on behalf of one another at any time. This is why the man Christ was able to say *I only do as I see my Father do.* Knowing we have been invited in to this same fellowship, we can begin to see our roles on this earth. *As He is so also are we,* as prophets, revealing the truth of the inclusion and invitation of mankind, as priests, presenting humanity as perfect, holy, blameless to themselves, and as kings, the rulers of this earthly realm. We are as David said in the Psalms.

Psalm 82:6 - *You are gods, And all of you are children of the Most High.*

We are not the creator of heaven and earth; but we are made of the same stuff as God – the very DNA of heaven. We are the lower case 'l, k, and g' in the statements Lord of lords, King of kings, and God of gods. He is the Supreme Being through whom all things were made; and we are members of His family, not subjects to His whims, but heirs to the throne! We are the life that His light gives life to!

CALEB MILLER

CHAPTER 12
FROM BREATH
TO BREATH
(OR DEATH TO DEATH)

"...the last Adam became a life giving spirit"
1 Corinthians 15:45

PREFACE:

I T IS ABSOLUTELY NECESSARY to understand the full nature of them who have dwelled together from before time began. The beginning of it all included something so few of us really grasp. Yet, it is the fundamental truth behind our very existence as sons of God. Earlier, we spoke briefly about the novelization of the bible. If the bible, as it is written now, were a novel, it would start with creation, end in destruction and have a large section in the middle about sin and redemption. It would have a God, who like a child at a beach building a sand castle, only builds it so He could destroy it at the end of the day. But it is not. It is pieced together sometimes chronologically and, sometimes just because the book seemed to fit best where they put it. If the bible were a novel however, I am convinced it would begin with John 1 - in the beginning was the word, the word was with God, the word was God and would end with the ascension of Christ. It would have a large section in the middle about the Father's commitment to mankind, the Son's love for humanity, and the Spirit's everlasting light shining on the whole thing.

FROM BREATH TO BREATH

John 1:1 (AMP) - *IN THE beginning [before all time] was the Word (Christ), and the Word was with God, and the Word was God Himself.*

In the beginning was the Word. This passage from John tells us what was going on before God created the heavens and the earth. I love the Amplified bible here. Before *all* time, before God ever set foot into the Garden of Eden, there was this word. That word was with God, and was God. The phrase *with God* means the two were sitting face to face, not just in the same location, but fixated on each other, not in narcissistic passion or sycophantic obsession, but in perfect fellowship. Then, the word became flesh. We understand the 'word' of this passage is the very person of the

Son. Before time existed, the Son dwelt with the Father in eternal fellowship with the Father and the Spirit; all existing as one - so close in fellowship that their thoughts flowed freely from one to another.

Before the creation of man there was the Word which was an inseparable part of God's very being and who was also His Son – the One destined to be offered up for our adoption. But God created Adam first; so this is where we start. The creation of Adam was something profound. God sat in the vast light of eternity, with angels, the Son, and the Spirit forever with Him, forever in fellowship and worship. Yet, He wanted something more; He wanted a family, and a legacy. From the narrative of creation we see that God speaks out of the depths of eternity, creates light, and thereby exposes the dark. He speaks and creates the seas, plants, and all animals. But with man, He takes a different approach.

Genesis 2:7 - *And the LORD God formed man of the dust of the ground, and breathed into his nostrils the breath of life; and man became a living being.*

The specifics of humanity's arrival on this earth are important. And for this section, we are going to deal with the fact that man was formed with God's own breath. God (and thereby the Word – the Son) spoke creation into existence; but He took the time and forethought to breathe life into Adam.

Do not all living things need breath? Animals breathe in and exhale, even plants have a sort of breathing process that takes place when they *inhale* carbon dioxide and *exhale* oxygen. So why did God take special care to breathe into Adam's lungs and not just speak him into existence like He did the other living things? Why was breath such an important part of humanity's creation?

FROM THE FOUNDATION OF THE WORLD

In the book of Revelation, Jesus is referred to as the Lamb slain from the foundation of the world. What is so important about this fact is the thought that Jesus was not the lamb slain from before there was time. It was as God was beginning His creation process, speaking things into existence that had yet to exist. He saw through the ages what would become of His son (Adam) and made the decision as one with the Son (Christ) to provide in advance for what was to come. Being one with the Son, they made the decision to provide a new blood line for the creation. Even as God was forming us with His breath, He had already decided to take on our identity as His own, and transform us into His. Look at what Paul says in the first few lines of Ephesians:

> Ephesians 1:4 (AMP) - *Even as [in His love] He chose us [actually picked us out for Himself as His own] in Christ before the foundation of the world, that we should be holy (consecrated and set*

apart for Him) and blameless in His sight, even above reproach, before Him in love.

Before the foundation of the world, He chose us in Him (Christ) before He even had the thought of creating us. This changes the game. It takes something away from access by confession, or at best forced guilt, and adds something to the message of His never ending, never questioned love for mankind!

Knowing what was to come, that it would be necessary for Christ to die in order for us to enter into the adoption He so eagerly provided, God formed man of the dust of the earth with His own breath. Remember, at this time, God and Christ are dwelling as one with the Holy Spirit. They are breathing together, giving life to the family God desired. As Adam comes to life with the breath of God inside him, the Word looks out through the ages, sees what is to come and what must be done in order to bring man back, before the fall has even happened. There is no small significance in the fact that Adam alone was formed from the breath of the Trinity. There is no small coincidence in the fact that nothing else was created this way. Merely a word from God, and all created things were made. But a breath from the Godhead was what started humanity's existence.

1 Corinthians 15:45 (AMP) - *Thus it is written, The first man Adam became a living being (an individual personality); the last Adam (Christ)* *became a life-giving Spirit [restoring the dead to life].*

In 1 Corinthians, Paul refers to Jesus as 'the last Adam' - Religion would have us to believe Adam is still very much alive and well in us, and we must die daily to Adam in order to receive of the Kingdom of Heaven. They dress it up with notions of a 'sin nature' but the truth is according to Paul is that Christ was the *last* Adam! Never again would mankind be subject to the whims of the flesh, because all had been changed upon the death of Christ.

We are told Christ became a life giving Spirit - restoring the dead (Genesis - dying you shall die) to life! - This *restoring to life* does not refer to a simple raising from the dead, but more accurately means *to produce alive, begat or bear young - to give life (as in birth)*. What happened? All of mankind was born in Christ. All of mankind were begotten by the begotten Son, to be Sons of the living God, brothers of the King, seated at the right hand of our Father with Christ! God used men and women who followed Christ on this earth to write the stories. We know the stories but all too often we skip over seemingly 'unimportant' details. There is truth between the lines and importance to things we would ignore.

Mark 15:37 (AMP) - *And Jesus uttered a loud cry, and breathed out His life*

It is no small coincidence that Jesus Christ, the Word who was in the beginning with God and as God, is recorded by Mark and Luke as having *breathed His last* upon His death on the cross. Just as Adam was formed using dust and the breath of the Word, the Word breathed his (Adam's) last upon the cross! Adam lay dead on the cross of Christ. Adam was buried in the tomb where they took the body of the Son. Adam stayed in the grave three days later when the Son of God came forth with defeat over Adam, sin, death and disease! By Adam here I mean the *nature* we have been taught is fallen. I believe that even Adam *the man* was raised to new life in Jesus Christ.

This phrasing here, *breathed out His life,* could literally read, *breathed out the breath of life.* Knowing the Word - Christ was with God in the beginning, breathed this same breath of life into man, means He breathed out the breath of life one last time. As if to sigh in relief that man had been brought back home, His very family was returned to their rightful place. He expelled the former breath and left it to die.

Hebrews 4:12 (AMP) - *For the Word that God speaks is alive and full of power [making it active, operative, energizing, and effective]; it is sharper than any two-edged sword, penetrating to the dividing line of the breath of life and [the immortal] spirit, and of joints and marrow [of the deepest parts of our nature], exposing and sifting* *and analyzing and judging the very thoughts and purposes of the heart.*

The words *penetrating to the dividing line* absolutely do no justice to the true meaning of what is taking place. The real meaning is *to cleave asunder or utterly separate.* Taking that into account, the Word (Christ) is alive and full of power - sharper than anything else - able to utterly separate the breath of life (Adam) and the immortal spirit (our new DNA)!

Take heart. Jesus was with God in the very beginning. The breath that gave Adam life is the same breath that ended the reign of flesh on this earth over 2000 years ago! Adam breathed his last, never to be raised again, never to be in power again, never to hold us back from our rightful place at God's right hand! What happened after the resurrection of Christ?

John 20:21-22 (AMP) - *Then Jesus said to them again, Peace to you! [Just] as the Father has sent Me forth, so I am sending you. And having said this, He breathed on them and said to them, receive the Holy Spirit!*

This is the third thing that happened after Christ rose from the dead. The first was His affirmation of Mary's identity (as He always did) and the second was His appearance to the disciples, showing His hands and side. Notice what Jesus says to them *just as the Father has sent me, so I am sending you.* We read things without taking note sometimes. These two - *sent* and *sending* are not synonyms. More than likely, we read this as some sort of commission for Christians that since God sent Christ here to heal, He is sending us to do the same. This is not the case! To grasp this we need to read further. *And having said this, He breathed on them and said, receive the Holy Spirit!* We cannot read *and having said this* without knowing what He said before. What was it He said? *As the Father has sent me, so I am sending you.* Now, we should look at those two words.

Sent – to order (one) to go to a place appointed – to send away, dismiss – to allow one to depart, that he may be in a state of liberty – to order one to depart, send off – to drive away.

God *sent* Christ into this world, into His appointed place, so he (we) may be in a state of liberty. Sending – to bid a thing to be carried to one – to send (thrust or insert) a thing into another. So, instead of a connotation of going out, this carries a deeper meaning of being thrust into – not out of.

What does this mean for us? Well, we ought to look at the verse again, using these meanings. *As the Father has sent me into this world, into My appointed place, that he (we) may be in a state of liberty, so I am bidding you to be carried and inserted into* - But inserted into what? Well, we should look at vs. 22 again. *And having said this, He breathed on them and said to them, receive the Holy Spirit!* - This particular phrasing - *breathed on them* - is only used one time in the entire Bible. It is the exact translation into the Greek that the Hebrew scholars used in talking about the creation of man in the beginning when God the Father, with the Word, *breathed* the breath of life into Adam! Receive is also an interesting word. What it means is this: to take upon and to take part in - or in other words, take now your part in, and be a part of the Holy Spirit.

So, this is what (I believe) Christ is saying. *As the Father has sent me into this world, into My appointed place, that he (we) may be in a state of liberty, so I am bidding you to be carried and inserted into the family of the Spirit, the very center of the Father, Son and Holy Spirit!*

And He did it all through His breath! In the beginning was the Word. The Word was with God, and the Word was God. The Word saw throughout the ages that man would need an avenue of adoption into the God life. So, He breathed the breath of life into man, in order that He would be the one in control of the end of the era of man and the beginning of the era of the new creation, the era of the God-Beings, the children of the same order and kind as the Father. Once He had breathed out the very same breath of life on the cross, and had risen again, once He had been living and active and divided the breath of life from the spirit, He used the same breath to insert man into His own family. By filling man with the Holy Spirit, He forever changed our makeup and DNA!

What does this mean for us? We are no longer subject to the whim and will of the flesh. We are subject to the power of the risen Son of God dwelling in us - and God in Him. We are subject to the very power of the Godhead -

three in one, working in us and through us and in fellowship with us. We are subject to the divine reversal of our very existence through their work.

CALEB MILLER

CHAPTER 13

THE PLAN FROM THE BEGINNING

"...he purposes in his sovereign will that all human history shall be consummated in Christ..."
Ephesians 1:10 PHILLIPS

GENESIS 1:28 - *THEN GOD BLESSED them, and God said to them, "Be fruitful and multiply; fill the earth and subdue it; have dominion over the fish of the sea, over the birds of the air, and over every living thing that moves on the earth."*

We began this little segment with the formation of man via the breath of God. The Father, Son, and Holy Spirit were together from the beginning; they looked into the ages and saw the need to involve breath in humanity's story. Then, they accomplished the need and fulfilled the use of humanity's breath on the cross.

With this approach, now we move on to God's first blessing of man (note that some might call this a command, but the actual words say *Then God blessed them and said...*) This is the first blessing: be fruitful, and multiply. Multiplication is the way God planned for His family to fill up the earth. Fill the earth - or replenish (according to the literal Hebrew) says this: consecrate the earth by filling it. This is a game changer. The intent from the beginning was for man not to dwell solely in the garden with God, but man, and thereby the garden, would multiply and cover the whole earth. The original intent through the Father's blessing was for the whole world to be consecrated through the multiplication of man.

The word multiply means to be or become great, to be or become many, to be or become much, to be or become numerous ... sort of like a 'divide and conquer' statement. Multiply can be translated as divide - make many, great, much, numerous of yourselves. I am belaboring the point; but I want to make it clear that God blessed Adam with the ability to become more than just one. God's blessing was for man to reproduce after his own kind and have multiple descendants for the initial filling and consecration of the earth.

Then, something happened. God had given this blessing of multiplication so man could divide himself and fill this earth. Then the fall took place, when man took the future of human existence into his own hands.

Before this happened God the Father, the Son and the Holy Spirit were together. They looked through the age, saw the fall and conspired to reverse it. Even as the creation of the universe was taking place, they discussed how to redeem the very family they were going to breathe into existence.

To understand the importance of multiplication, we need to understand what happened to man through the division of the ages.

> **Genesis 11:6-8** - *And the LORD said, "Indeed the people [are] one and they all have one language, and this is what they begin to do; now nothing that they propose to do will be withheld from them. "Come, let Us go down and there confuse their language, that they may not understand one another's speech." So the LORD scattered them abroad from there over the face of all the earth, and they ceased building the city.*

The descendants of Adam, who were already so numerous they were in a position to build a tower to heaven, had all begun to gather into one place to become one. God Himself says they are one, and because of it, nothing they propose to do will be withheld from them. What is being played out is a foreshadowing that which is to come. The Father, Son, and Holy Spirit stand outside of time, looking at things on a plane we cannot understand. They see the people as one and give us an idea of the ability oneness can produce, and its inability to fail.

But the time was not right. Consequently the Father, seeing how they had ignored the blessing of *fill the earth*, decides to passively *force* them to fill the earth by confusing their language. This passive action causes man to spread out, thereby fulfilling the original blessing of the Father. God has always been about mankind receiving blessing. He has always been about mankind receiving all that He intended them to receive.

So man begins to move outward. They are filling the earth, multiplying. As they do this, events begin to take place that will forever change the makeup of human history.

The stories of the Old Testament refer to humanity's scattering over 70 times. Throughout the timeline of man, there is disobedience, followed by scattering, followed by gathering, and repeating the whole cycle. This says two things about God. One - any blessing He gives is without repeal; He told man to multiply and fill the earth. This is exactly what they are doing; and two, His plan for man was and is for our total habitation of this planet. Too many seem to believe we are destined for heaven, when the bible clearly says there is a new heaven and a new earth to come. The two will be one. We are not going to discuss this yet though. Just know, if it is to come, it has to be now, too. Heaven and earth are already together, existing in unity - whether we experience it or not.

The Father's intent was filling the earth, and through the filling of the earth, its consecration. The consecration of this earth by humanity's multiplication was His intended will.

But there is this fall we keep running into. And God, who was with Christ from the beginning, saw it before He breathed into Adam. So Christ set out to utterly reverse the fall before its full brunt had been felt. Even before the bite of fruit hit the belly of man, the plan had been set in motion to remove the effect of the fall and provide all human history with an atonement and adoption. However, man seemed bent on scattering.

THE ROAD TO CONSUMMATION

Now, mankind is wandering through this world trying desperately to attain to something God blessed them to be - holy. They are forever searching for who they are, the real identity crisis of *where do we belong?* During their time in the wilderness, an event happens that forever changes the way they approach God. The Law is introduced. No longer do they approach Him as Father, Creator and Friend. They begin to approach Him as God, Holy, Righteous, Just, and Judgmental.

It is not the Father who changes His approach. It is mankind who changes in their approach of Him. God wanted Fatherhood of His family. He wanted to be the light in the darkness, the cloud in the daytime, and their protection from the world at large. But they decided Moses should be the one to talk to GOD for them, instead of speaking with Father themselves.

The Father, Son and Spirit had conspired from the beginning to save all humanity and bring them all into the family. This leads us to Ephesians.

Ephesians 1:7-10 (PHILLIPS) - *It is through the Son, at the cost of his own blood, that we are redeemed, freely forgiven through that full and generous grace which has overflowed into our lives and opened our eyes to the truth. For God had allowed us to know the secret of his plan, and it is this: he purposes in his sovereign will that all human history shall be consummated in Christ, that everything that exists in Heaven or earth shall find its perfection and fulfillment in him.*

The religious would have us to believe Paul is writing just to Christians in this passage. I purposely chose the J.B. Phillips translation because I believe it paints a perfect image of what God intended from the beginning. Paul says God has allowed us (Paul's church at Ephesus) to know the secret of His plan, that all human history - *all human history!!!* - would be consummated in Christ. We have already showed that all human history means all past, all present, and all future!

We have been leading up to this. When the Father, the Son, and the Spirit were creating the cosmos, their intention from the very beginning was to usher mankind into adoption. This adoption means something so much more than just becoming a son; it means becoming *one* with the very Godhead. To the culture of the day, adoption was a process by which even a blood-born child was given the rights of the familial relationship. Paul knew this and took liberty to use their terminology. The literal word used for consummated means *to sum up again, to condense into a summary.* We have literally become one through the act of Christ's sacrifice. We have all been consummated in Him!

To explore this a little deeper, we must look back to how God originally blessed man and said - *be fruitful, multiply and fill the earth - replenish it* or *consecrate it.* Where man fell, Christ has utterly and completely reversed the fall. Originally, we were blessed and told to make the whole earth holy by our multiplication. Christ's reversal was this: He has made the whole earth holy by His consummation of humanity, or the reverse-multiplication of mankind. God had told us to spread out; and now because of His Son, He has brought us all back together as one with Him, one with His Son, and one with His spirit to live the life He had always intended.

We talked earlier about the power of what Jesus said when He was hanging on the cross. We know this phrase as *it is finished,* and this phrase carries something great with it. But, the Spanish translation really nails it *consumado es.* What is finished? The consummation of all human history!

The high point of human history is not the cross of Christ, but the person of Christ. Everything that happened to Israel in the Old Testament was a type of what happens when God makes covenant with man. There is a necessary reworking of human flesh when it is in covenant with perfection and love. That love causes bumps which must be reworked. What does this mean for us? Everything Israel went through was leading forward to the person of Christ; He was the summation of the Old, and going forward He is the consummation of all human history! The Father made covenant with Jesus Christ, reworking Him for our sakes, so we would never need to be reworked again. Jesus is the high point of all human history, the very pinnacle of our existence; and in Him we find our fulfillment and perfection! His incarnation signified the end of covenantal language between God and man, and showed a new covenant between God and God.

CHAPTER 14
UNASHAMED

"And they were both naked, the man and his wife, and were not ashamed."
Genesis 2:25

TO COMPLETELY UNDERSTAND all that Jesus provided with this divine reversal we are talking about, we have to fully grasp what happened at the fall. There was so much more than just a simple act of disobedience, so much greater a tragedy than humanity's removal from the garden. Man had given up who he really was and lost his identity with its fruit plus all it was meant to bring to this earth. The Father, Son, and Spirit were together and witnessed when the greatest tragedy to ever befall man took place … in one instant the lie that humanity could do something to become more like God.

We have to discuss this fall. We cannot believe for one moment God was upset with mankind for the action of the fall. It was not the disobedience. It was not lying about who ate first or even the fact they listened to the voice of accusation. The Father watched as the creation He had been walking with in the cool of the day did something so unthinkable, so destructive to his very being, it would change forever the course of human history.

"God knows that the day you eat of it, you will become more like Him"

This phrase would not only change the approach of man; but it would begin the lie that would spiral into what the world would call sin. The fact mankind, who was created in the very expressed image of God, in the likeness of the Son, with the same DNA as the Spirit, would think there was anything he could do to be more like these three with whom he already had deep fellowship, was something unfathomable. The Father had put into man all He possessed except one small detail. In most "grace" circles we have been taught we were created with nothing lacking, nothing missing. However, we were in fact created without one small thing, which religion and humanity immediately force upon us from the day we are able to understand. That small thing is the knowledge of good and evil. We call it right and wrong, moral and immoral, good and bad etc. A better way of saying this is separation. We were created with no knowledge of separation.

You see, only the Father was meant to determine such a difference. It was never for us to know. We were never to attempt to make the distinction between the two. If we never knew, we would know only good. There is none good but God according to Christ; knowing that, we should stay our eyes upon Him with the result of knowing good. But we focus on the negative. We judge what is evil and good. We use scripture as our back up while we blow up abortion clinics and picket in front of them, yet do not realize the man performing these acts is a man who has been included into the life of the Father, Son and Spirit, with the same divine light running through him. He has probably never been told this and each time we stand outside, knowing good from evil, we distance him further from the only thing that will set him free - a life of fellowship with the Father. We use a lie of morality to bully those of whom we disapprove into a life we can more easily control. To teach morality is to teach heresy, because morality is of your own making. If I rather teach the risen Christ in you and you in Him, your moral conduct will follow suit, without me saying a word about it.

Rather than helping people who are in the deepest, darkest parts of a massive identity crisis to realize the truth of who they are we make a decision. We determine good from evil, perpetuate the fall, and make much of the identity crisis. It has gotten so great that there are people all over this earth searching in every religion, every intellectual thought, and every humanist tradition for meaning. They want to know the meaning of life, when all along it has been right in front of them.

We have all, (and in saying all, I mean every person who walks this earth, every person who ever has walked this earth, and every person who ever will), been included into the life of the Father, and the fellowship He shares with His Son, and the Holy Spirit. This truth is something deeper than we will ever fully grasp with our finite minds; it is what Paul was talking about when he said, "for now we know in part". We are here as ministers of reconciliation, as those who profess the name of the Son as their identity, to help awaken others to this fact.

So what happened at the beginning? Mankind was created with the innate ability to fellowship one on one with the Father, walk with Him in the cool of the day and enjoy the very manifest presence of the One who would later be feared and misunderstood. Yet even in this fellowship, where man was meant to look at the Father and assume that he looked the same way, the mirror became skewed with the lie of something he could do to become more like that which he already was.

If the serpent had been less cunning, it would have said something like "He knows that in eating this, you will become more like yourself" - that line never would have flown. Adam would have understood he could not be more like who he already was; so the lie began with this idea of becoming more like God. In an instant, the One who had been known as Father & Friend became God & King.

Genesis 2:25 - *And they were both naked, the man and his wife, and were not ashamed.*

This verse has been interpreted to say they were not ashamed of their nakedness. This is true; but it is only a partial truth. These are two separate thoughts. Our minds like to say they were not ashamed to be undressed, but the larger picture here is these are attributes of Adam and Eve. They were naked. And they had no shame in them, either about their nakedness, or about themselves.

And then the fall. Man had not known what shame was until this moment in history. They had bought the lie of something they could do to become more like who they already were. They had swallowed the idea that God had made them less than perfect and in that belief came what we can never know the way they knew it. This is what real shame is. Shame is looking into the eyes of the Father and feeling like you are not measuring up. It is looking at the beauty He is and then looking to ourselves and realizing (wrongly) we do not look the same way He does.

> **Genesis 3:10** - *So he said, "I heard Your voice in the garden, and I was afraid because I was naked; and I hid myself." And He said, "Who told you that you were naked? Have you eaten from the tree of which I commanded you that you should not eat?"*

We have to understand something about shame. Real shame comes only from one place, and that is a place comparing us to 'God' (not in the light of "Father"). When we are under shame, fear sets in. Do we see what happened to Adam? They were with God in the beginning, naked and unashamed. Then, they ate of the tree of knowledge of good and evil and instantly shame set in on them, which brought fear. They were ashamed of who they were and what they looked like; and in their own eyes, the fact they did not look like the Father. They began to look to self and see they had a different physical appearance than their Father, and in an instant went from naked (unafraid) and unashamed to afraid and ashamed.

Now, we can only feel the effects of shame when we compare ourselves to "God" and through that comparison are afraid of God and what He might do "when He finds out what we have done". If you are feeling shame in your life today, I want you to know there is freedom, because what we have done was forever paid in full at the Cross of Jesus Christ.

In the literal meaning of shame, we find this little word *disgraced*.

DISGRACED

There are no words that penetrate the heart deeper than the words of "you are not good enough, you are a disgrace". The idea of being disgraced brings fear to any in leadership, whether in church or in the work world. From the start, man was not meant to know this feeling. All we were ever meant to know was the truth of our relationship with the Father.

Disgraced has this meaning of being injured, hurt physically and emotionally. It is something much deeper than just an emotional hurt, something deeper than what we would call shame in our language. To the Hebrew though, it is a part of shame.

The prophet Isaiah had a partial grasp on the beauty of what Jesus would accomplish for man.

Isaiah 45:17 - *But Israel shall be saved by the LORD With an everlasting salvation; You shall not be ashamed or disgraced Forever and ever.*

He saw into the ages of man what was going to happen in the death, burial, and resurrection of the Son, and what that meant for humanity. He said in one verse something we have failed to grasp: *You shall not be ashamed or disgraced forever and ever.* For all eternity, the Father was making a statement through Isaiah that there was to be NO MORE FEAR of what He would do to mankind for their actions! He was putting an end to fear and the shame it produces. And, He was making a statement about this physical shame - disgrace - would be put to an end, also.

We need to understand what the Father is saying: no longer - never again, should you expect hurt, physical, emotional or otherwise. No longer should you expect injury for your actions, because I am going to lay that physical pain upon my Son. Jesus Christ bore our sicknesses, carried our diseases, and the chastisement for our peace was upon Him!

We have been graced - the dis has been removed, and forever placed behind the (locked) gates of hell. Jesus left it there when He descended to the depths to take our place, never to be seen again.

DISHONORED

The next part of humanity's shame was the idea of being dishonored. The Father had done something for man that David knew when he penned the Psalm "*who is man....for thou hast crowned him with glory and honor*". The Father's own honor had been given to mankind for a crown. Man knew of this honor and the very reason David had it in his heart. No idea is new to humanity's heart except what was already there from the beginning. God gave us all things, save one, the knowledge of self. Our honor from the beginning was an honor only the Father, Son, and Holy Spirit could bestow. The three who had created all things and dwelt together from before time existed, crowned mankind with this honor.

Honor is something greater than importance. It means glory and majesty. In essence, what we were (and are again) crowned with is the very glory and majesty of the Trinity. Man was created to be a part of the life of the Father, Son and Holy Spirit. To be a part of that life is to be clothed in glory and crowned with majesty.

We have placed much importance on the fact that man was dishonored; when in fact, the word *dishonored* occurs only a handful of times in the literal versions of the bible. The word dishonored is mentioned in **Leviticus 20:11** when the law was given. This particular instance refers to the dishonoring of a father by a child sleeping with his wife.

This word has an amazing literal translation though. The literal passage says *He has uncovered His nakedness.*

The fall did just that; it gave man the idea they were not clothed the same way as the Father and looked differently. As David saw, nothing could have been further from the truth; nevertheless, the lie had set in. In his own mind, man had become dishonored. The Father had never removed the crown of glory and honor; but humanity had taken the lie and thereby, removing it from themselves.

Something we need to take into account when dealing with the idea of dishonor is the passage in 2 Timothy 2:20 that speaks of vessels of honor, and vessels of dishonor: there are vessels that have come to the knowledge of their clothing, and vessels that have not. Where man lost that honor in his own mind during the fall, the Father has replaced it for us. Where man realized his nakedness, the Father has clothed us once again with glory. God does not create vessels of dishonor in the way we think of them. He creates vessels who through life's walk and realize their nakedness before Him. Then, by awakening them to righteousness, He honors them again; and they can see they are clothed in glory!

Understanding our seated position with Christ brings a new revelation of our place in Him. Jesus said in John that He honored His Father, and His Father honored Him. What we have to grasp and important for us to understand is if we are seated in the heavens with Him, then the same honor the Father has bestowed upon the Son has also been bestowed upon us!

DISCREDITED

The enemy loves nothing more than discrediting the finished work of Jesus Christ. The religious world does much of his work for him; so he is able to focus on the task of lying. We live our lives with a total misunderstanding of all that Christ accomplished for us. We pursue fruit instead of pursuing the seed that produces the fruit. To steal a phrase from another teacher, we reach into the refrigerator for the pizza instead of realizing the depths of the fact we are even in the kitchen!

Man had been given credit from before there was even a thought of creation. He had been predestined for adoption from before the foundation of the world. The Father, Son and Spirit had conspired together to create a family; and in creating that family, to offer us adoption into their own life. The credit was there. Man had been instilled with an initial credit, an account of the Father's giving. It is the *fill the earth and subdue it* credit we discussed earlier. Already, we talked about how through mankind's filling the earth, it would present the earth as holy. Now though, we need to realize something. Man was created to have the authority on this earth; and that credit of authority was given up in our own minds when the fall happened. Today, many of us still live as though we are under the fall, or that this world is still fallen. IT IS NOT a fallen world! This world is a redeemed world that just does not know it yet!

The idea of discredited is contained in the word shame. To be discredited means the original gift was taken away. Humanity's authority was so great that just in thinking the authority was gone, the authority left. We do not understand the power of the credit the Father bestowed upon us. Our authority is so great; even humanistic, self-help gurus understand the mind is a powerful healing mechanism. Apart from medicine and science, there is viable proof of people who continue to believe they are healthy, and therefore remain healthy.

So where does this leave us?

We were counted with Christ on the cross, among the dead when Christ entered the tomb. Now, we are counted among the living and have been re-credited. There are very few references to this thought in the word, but the Greek meaning of the word credit is fantastic. Credit means *glory*!

Jesus Christ has forever credited us and restored the glory and honor with which we were originally crowned, once and for all to reverse the effect of the fall, and take us to a place far greater than the place just before the fall. He has taken us back to the *restart*; back to the place where the Father had the idea of creation. He has utterly and completely reversed everything.

CHAPTER 15

THE MESSAGE FROM THE START

"We religious are those who walk down hallways filled with fine art, looking for a mirror" – Wm. Paul Young

T HE EFFECT OF THE FALL sent shockwaves throughout human history. It forever changed the course of human events, how we would approach our Father, and how we would live in regards to religion, personal life, and all other aspects. The One who had been known as Father and Friend, would come to be feared as God and King. We have this belief that when man was removed from the garden, the Father stayed behind, as though to hide Himself from the sin that had invaded creation.

Genesis 3:23-24 - *therefore the LORD God sent him out of the garden of Eden to till the ground from which he was taken. So He drove out the man; and He placed cherubim at the east of the garden of Eden, and a flaming sword which turned every way, to guard the way to the tree of life.*

Genesis 4:6 - *So the LORD said to Cain, "Why are you angry? And why has your countenance fallen?*

Did you see what happened here?

The Lord said to Cain. This is not some prophetic word spoken in Cain's heart. It is the very Father, speaking audibly, face to face with this "sinner". We must grasp that the Father did not stay behind the door of the garden. Until the creation of the temple, He had no other dwelling place other than among mankind. He did not place an angel at the gate, and then stand at a distance. He entered into humanity's darkness before the incarnation of the Son, and dwelt with us - in our sin. This is vastly important, because religion would tell us that the Father cannot abide sin. He can and did, and continues to do so. In order to become sin for us, He had to put it on; He had to be able to abide it. We cannot think for one second that the Father stood away, holy, un-approachable, and, in His utter *untouchability* spoke things to us from afar. He dwelt alongside man. He loved man, followed man into the depths of darkness, and walked with him out of that darkness.

The Father does not despise our humanity. In fact, the Father was so terribly and utterly smitten with humanity, He conspired within Himself to become human, to experience the human life and all our darkness, pain, sadness and distress. Now we have a human being seated at the right hand of the Father! To say the Father despises the *flesh* of humanity is to say He despises His own Son, who is still living in a flesh and blood body.

EXILED

We have this mindset that we are exiled, banished from the Father's presence, until the day we accept Jesus Christ as our personal Lord and Savior. Like we are enemies until we believe. Listen to this: even the devils believe! What does this say?

1. There is no acceptance needed for Him to be the Lord.
2. There is no belief necessary for Him to be the Savior.

Religion tries to make it about how much we believe; or we truly believe He is who He says He is. Our belief is important, but like everything else, our belief is a fruit of properly understood placement in the courts of the Father. Until we understand we are placed at His right hand, we simply can never make the jump out of that place of exile. The little bit we have to bring to this equation will sneak into it. Listen carefully: Mankind has nothing to bring to the table of salvation. If it is not all Him, it is not Him at all! This is powerful. The Son once and for all provided our salvation, and all of mankind's salvation, over 2,000 years ago. He forever bore all mankind in Himself on the cross, left Adam in the grave, and created a new kind of being when He rose again with us inside of Him. Our faith is merely a response of belief to the faith *of* Jesus Christ. - Paul's statement in Galatians was a positional one; we are *in* the faith *of* Jesus Christ.

> **Isaiah 51:14 (AMP)** - *The captive exile and he who is bent down by chains shall speedily be released; and he shall not die and go down to the pit of destruction, nor shall his food fail.*

Isaiah is prophesying about the coming Messiah. He is giving us a view of what Jesus is going to accomplish at the cross. Look at this: the captive exile shall be speedily released, and he shall not die! He shall not go down to the pit of destruction!

We need to dig into this verse a bit. Something is missed here at first glance - though the verse is powerful on its own. The captive exile is anyone who is bent low, in chains, or feels as though they are held captive by something. This is the world at large. It is those who feel as though we live in a fallen world, and are daily trying to put Adam to death and do Christ's job. Speedily is not something we grasp. It is a quick and sudden release. It is freedom all at once - with no delay. He shall not die and go down to the pit of destruction - who shall not? The captive exile.

I want to put all this together, because an unseen power is here. What Isaiah is prophesying is this, those who feel as though they are exiled, your freedom will be once for all, and neither the grave, nor hell, can hold you.

This speedy freedom....this means with no delay. We live as though freedom has taken (so far) over 2000 years to come to fruition. But what Isaiah is telling us is freedom was enacted at this one specific time in history. At one point, with one fatal blow, Christ ended the attitude of the exile and brought us forward to something greater.

I want to make something clear. It is not as though the Father were bound by natural law; however, there is a principal in physics regarding fire. Fire cannot burn where fire has already burned, meaning this: with no fuel, source of spark, or oxygen, fire cannot exist. We have this great authority on earth to breathe our breath of life into things that Christ forever put to death. Things like sin, sickness, disease, and devils. Devils? Yes. Christ won the victory once and for all. We like to have something to blame though, so we either attribute things to the "sovereignty of God" or "evil spirits". Did Jesus defeat the enemy? Yes. Do we revive him with our breath of complaint, gossip, and credit giving? Yes. That is the oxygen that can spread a fire quickly. Our air spreads the fires of hell. The fuel this fire is trying to consume is us. We must grasp the fullness of Christ in us, and us in Him. It is paramount. When we understand this truth, the fire cannot go where it is already been. Add that together with the fact that we have a risen Savior who has already been through the fire. We cannot be burned. As Isaiah put it we will *not die and go down to the pit.*

This is why it is so important to teach the message of our inclusion into the life of the Father. When we fully grasp what we have been brought into, every pursuit of life will become a fruit of the Holy Spirit in which we dwell. If Jesus Christ is the One in and through and by whom all things were made, then all things have just become a part of who we are. When it is a part of who we are, it is a natural fruit of the life of the Father, Son and Holy Spirit flowing through us. I cannot help but pour out love if I am dwelling in that life. I cannot help but walk in health if I am dwelling in that life. I cannot help but give if I am dwelling in that life.

Once we understand the idea that any type of exile is done away with, where do we go from here?

INCLUDED

Paul was the guy. He was the one who spent time alone with Christ in the wilderness and received the message of grace directly from the mouth of Him who had created all things. We need a little back-story to this letter though. The Roman church had been filled with Jews and Gentiles together; Paul's letter deals with this issue. The Jewish believers had begun to force the Gentiles to observe the law. In the midst of all this, there was also idol worship beginning to infiltrate the Roman church.

Paul begins his letter, as he did most, by just simply introducing himself and giving his title. But then, he immediately goes into vs. 3

Romans 1:3 (NLT) - *the good news is about His Son...*

He is setting the stage for what this is really all about. It is all about Christ. Then in vs. 5 he makes it known what his ministry call is:

Romans 1:5-6 (NLT) - *Through Christ, God has given us the privilege and authority as apostles to tell Gentiles everywhere what God has done for them, so that they will believe and obey him, bringing glory to his name. And you are included among those Gentiles who have been called to belong to Jesus Christ.*

You are included! What is Paul saying here? He is saying Jews, Romans and Gentiles, ALL are called and INCLUDED among those who belong to Jesus Christ. This is not a doctrine of Calvinist election; it is a truth of what the Father wanted. Look now at Peter's sermon in Acts:

Acts 3:25 (NLT) - *You are the children of those prophets, and you are included in the covenant God promised to your ancestors. For God said to*

Abraham, 'Through your descendants all the families on earth will be blessed.

Peter is speaking to the Jews who are around who have just witnessed healing by the name of Christ. What is the first message he gives these people? Condemnation, sin, sexual conduct? No, YOU ARE INCLUDED! He wants them to know that they are included also.

The message of our inclusion into the life of the Father is the very seed on which we need to focus. Without this truth, every pursuit of life is just that, a pursuit. However, when we focus on our inclusion, and let that seed grow, the fruit will produce itself. As a result, we will no longer wander around waiting for some miracle to happen. It will be an effortless change!

The unconditional nature of grace is offensive to the mind of man. The acceptance and love of the Father is something in which we long to have a part. We act as though contributing our will (free will does not appear in the written word) creates our place of inclusion. It simply does not. The sacrifice of the Son made the road for our inclusion and was given without requirement, sacrifice or repentance.

T.F. Torrance said it this way; *The voice of divine forgiveness and the voice of divine judgment are one and the same (The Mediation of Christ).* Jesus said in John 4 *the Father judges no one, but has given all judgment to the Son.* The judgment Jesus offered was a judgment of divine forgiveness. This forgiveness was either once and for the whole of the human race, or it was not for any one. Everyone has been included in this one act of divine judgment; and everyone has been offered forgiveness.

Religion continually tries to tell us that we have something to add to the equation, that through our acceptance of the truth of Christ we are saved, or through our belief, or through any other activity of life.

Take a look at Paul's statement in Ephesians:

Ephesians 2:1-9 - *And you [He made alive], who were dead in trespasses and sins, in which you once walked according to the course of this world, according to the prince of the power of the air, the spirit who now works in the sons of disobedience, among whom also we all once conducted ourselves in the lusts of our flesh, fulfilling the desires of the flesh and of the mind, and were by nature children of wrath, just as the others. But God, who is rich in mercy, because of His great love with which He loved us, even when we were dead in trespasses, made us alive together with Christ (by grace you have been saved), and raised [us] up together, and made [us] sit together in the heavenly [places] in Christ Jesus, that in the ages to come He might show the exceeding riches of His grace in [His] kindness toward us in Christ Jesus. For by grace you have been saved through faith, and that not of yourselves; [it is] the gift of God, not of works, lest anyone should boast.*

Paul does something to utterly smash the heart of religion. He says in this one simple passage salvation came while he and his church in Ephesus were dead in their flesh. Before they had ever acknowledged it, they had been included into this fellowship. Verses 8-9 perfectly sum up the whole thought, *not of yourselves, not of works, but it is the gift of God.* Paul says over in Romans 11:29 that the gifts of God are *irrevocable*. This word *irrevocable* means not repented of. It means this, that the gift of God, salvation, was given freely to all mankind. God's not changing His mind about that!

Ephesians 2:11-22 (PHILLIPS) - *Do not lose sight of the fact that you were born "Gentiles", known by those whose bodies were circumcised as "the uncircumcised". You were without Christ, you were utter strangers to God's chosen community, the Jews, and you had no knowledge of, or right to, the promised agreements. You had nothing to look forward to and no God to whom you could turn. But now, through the blood of Christ, you who were once outside the pale are with us inside the circle of God's love and purpose. For Christ is our living peace. He has made a unity of the conflicting elements of Jew and Gentile by breaking down the barrier which lay between us. By his sacrifice he removed the hostility of the Law, with all its commandments and rules, and made in himself out of the two, Jew and Gentile, one new man, thus producing peace. For he reconciled both to God by* *the sacrifice of one body on the cross, and by this act made utterly irrelevant the antagonism between them. Then he came and told both you who were far from God and us who were near that the war was over. And it is through him that both of us now can approach the Father in the one Spirit. So you are no longer outsiders or aliens, but fellow-citizens with every other Christian—you belong now to the household of God. Firmly beneath you in the foundation, God's messengers and prophets, the actual foundation-stone being Jesus Christ himself. In him each separate piece of building, properly fitting into its neighbor, grows together into a temple consecrated to God. You are all part of this building in which God himself lives by his spirit.*

The Master Artist painted a beautiful picture with His atonement and purchase. He laid something out for us that would forever end our exile with one simple phrase:

You.

Are.

Included.

Stop looking for a mirror to see yourself and start looking into that which you have been included.

CALEBMILLER

CHAPTER 16
FROM FALL
TO ASCENSION

*"Now this, "He ascended"--what does it mean but that He also
first descended into the lower parts of the earth?"*
Ephesians 4:9

W E HAVE COVERED MUCH ground in all that Jesus
accomplished in reversing the effects of the fall. We
need to grasp what Christ did; He did not simply
remove guilt and leave us in a fallen state. He did not simply
give us the avenue for adoption, and leave us at the
orphanage (even though we have always been His children).
No! Jesus Christ not only became our avenue of adoption,
but brought us home to our Father, and forever removed us

from the tyranny of the one who had implanted the identity crisis that led to the fall in the first place. He has utterly and completely reversed the fall. Therefore, we are no longer in a fallen state, but live in a place of resurrection, new life, and total right standing with God, a state of *righteousness.*

To accurately understand all that Christ did, first we must understand the importance of one name He was given by Paul, which is "The Last Adam". The very phrase Paul uses says a number of things for us today. Jesus was not the *second* Adam, nor was He just *another* Adam, but most importantly, He was the *last* Adam. This means no more Adams from Jesus onward. But today, we live like we are still putting Adam to death by crucifying our flesh, denying ourselves, etc. Also, the fact He was called the last *Adam* carries much weight. He could have been called the last *Deity,* the last *Virgin Born son of Man,* or any other title by which we may know Him; but yet, we have the last Adam as the name of Christ.

So what is the importance of all this? To fully grasp the power of this *last Adam,* we need to look to the truths in the word about the first Adam.

> **Romans 5:12-21** - *Therefore, just as through one man sin entered the world, and death through sin, and thus death spread to all men, because all sinned— 13 (For until the law sin was in the world, but sin is not imputed when there is no law. 14 Nevertheless death reigned from Adam to Moses, even over those who had not sinned*

according to the likeness of the transgression of Adam, who is a type of Him who was to come. 15 But the free gift is not like the offense. For if by the one man's offense many died, much more the grace of God and the gift by the grace of the one Man, Jesus Christ, abounded to many. 16 And the gift is not like that which came through the one who sinned. For the judgment which came from one offense resulted in condemnation, but the free gift which came from many offenses resulted in justification. 17 For if by the one man's offense death reigned through the one, much more those who receive abundance of grace and of the gift of righteousness will reign in life through the One, Jesus Christ.) 18 Therefore, as through one man's offense judgment came to all men, resulting in condemnation, even so through one Man's righteous act the free gift came to all men, resulting in justification of life. 19 For as by one man's disobedience many were made sinners, so also by one Man's obedience many will be made righteous. 20 Moreover the law entered that the offense might abound. But where sin abounded, grace abounded much more, 21 so that as sin reigned in death, even so grace might reign through righteousness to eternal life through Jesus Christ our Lord.

This passage perfectly sums up the work of Adam on this earth. It is his biography as it were. Paul takes special care in defining what Adam accomplished. It is clearly stated that through the man Adam, death came to all people because of Adam's sin. In the same fashion, righteousness came to all people through the last Adam, Jesus. V 18 says this:

> *Therefore, as through one man's offense judgment came to all men, resulting in condemnation, even so through one Man's righteous act the free gift came to all men, resulting in justification of life.*

Did we read this like it is really written, or place our own religious requirement into it? Paul says the free gift came to all people, resulting in justification of life. Because of the sacrifice of Christ, all people are now justified and pure before the Father!

The words *even so* in this passage carry much weight. They mean something far greater than our English words convey. The literal meaning of *even so* is this: *in the same fashion as what was previously stated.* Now we will use that and go through this passage again. *Through the one man death entered and spread to all, in the same fashion justification of life came to all through the free gift.* This changes things a bit! This is something we need to understand. Were people required to accept their inclusion into Adam? Did they have to confess their belief in Adam's failure in order to be lumped in to his situation? No! Simply by being born on this earth, they were included into the death Adam had introduced. In the same fashion, the free gift has been given to ALL PEOPLE, resulting in the justification of life for ALL PEOPLE! This is important to grasp because unless we understand what Paul is really saying, we leave ourselves holding something in our salvation equation.

Paul does make the point here to say something about reception; and I believe it is worth touching:

> V17 *For if by the one man's offense death reigned through the one, much more those who receive abundance of grace and of the gift of righteousness will reign in life through the One, Jesus Christ.*

He tells us the purpose of the acceptance and reception of the grace of God - reigning in life! This says a couple things to me. One, our acceptance of the matter does not gain us access to heaven and freedom from hell; and two, if we are not reigning in life, then we have not received grace in that area of our lives! It is a simple association. Paul says those who receive the gift of righteousness *will* reign in life, not *might,* or *can,* but *will!* Reign is a powerful word. It means to be king or to exercise kingly power! If I am not reigning in some area, I can rest because in order to change the situation around, the only thing necessary is to receive the gift of righteousness! Right now, in what area of your life are you not exercising your kingly power? Receive grace!

Consequently, through the first Adam, sin came to all people, and death reigned. Now we look to the last Adam, Jesus Christ. Remember what we have discovered about Adam as we move into Paul's letter to the Corinthians.

1 Corinthians 15:42-49 - *So also is the resurrection of the dead. The body is sown in corruption, it is raised in incorruption. 43 It is sown in dishonor, it is raised in glory. It is sown in weakness, it is raised in power. 44 It is sown a natural body, it is raised a spiritual body. There is a natural body, and there is a spiritual body. 45 And so it is written, "The first man Adam became a living being." The last Adam became a life-giving spirit. 46 However, the spiritual is not first, but the natural, and afterward the spiritual. 47 The first man was of the earth, made of dust; the second Man is the Lord from heaven. 48 As was the man of dust, so also are those who are made of dust; and as is the heavenly Man, so also are those who are heavenly. 49 And as we have borne the image of the man of dust, we shall also bear the image of the heavenly Man.*

Paul is saying something about the finished work of the last Adam. Through the laying down of flesh as seed, an incorruptible, perfect seed was allowed to germinate. (In Verse 37, Paul says *And what you sow, you do not sow that body that shall be, but mere grain—perhaps wheat or some other grain.)* He is making this association that the first Adam must be sown into the ground, the very tomb of Christ. As a result, the last Adam can be raised up and grant perfection to all. Something is lost in the translation in verse 49. The phrase *we shall also bear* is literally *so also we bear*. This is much different than some future tense promise. We are here, bearing the very image of the heavenly man! Paul says that the first Adam became a living being and the last a life-giving spirit. We need to grasp something about man and God here. Everything man is, does and creates generates a need. Conversely, everything God is, does and creates fills a need. Think of it naturally for a few seconds. Man creates automobiles, which need gas, oil, water, air, and electricity, all just to run. God created oil, water, air and electricity! Adam created the need for re-creation; God re-created! Adam created death; God answered that need by incarnating His son to die our death for us! Paul says in Romans that if one died for all, then all died. Jesus Christ died for all, leaving all no choice but to die with Him, co-crucified with Him. The power of it all is that Jesus did not do what Adam did, leaving humanity dead in the garden; He left Adam dead in the tomb, raising humanity up with Himself in newness of life, in the power of His resurrection.

Jesus has given the whole of humanity justification of life, in the same fashion as Adam gave to all people sin and death. There is nothing you can do about it; you are justified and righteous! Receive your new life and walk in the abundance thereof, but never think that our reception makes us new, righteous, holy, or justified. Christ took care of that for us!

We need to relate this back to the fall to fully understand what Jesus accomplished.

> **Ephesians 4:9-10** - *(Now this, "He ascended"-- what does it mean but that He also first descended into the lower parts of the earth? He who descended is also the One who ascended far above all the heavens, that He might fill all things.)*

We understand that Jesus ascended, and this fact is of supreme importance because without ascension, we do not have a high priest seated at the right hand of the Father or a human sitting in our place in the throne room this very second. However, just as important as His ascending is His descending. Without descending, ascending would hold little importance or power. To have a man who simply died, rose again, and went to heaven means the single most important step in our redemption was left behind. This is the step: His descent into the very depths of hell, to the place where the devil and his angels were, and taking from the devil something so critical to our existence was the very reason Jesus came in the first place.

I want to jump back a verse to see why Jesus needed to descend, or at least what is being said here in Ephesians about His descension.

Ephesians 4:8 - *Therefore He says: "When He ascended on high, He led captivity captive, And gave gifts to men."*

The purpose of His descending was so He could lead captivity captive. This carries profound weight. The literal word for captivity is both the place of captivity and the one who leads people there. So what was said is that Christ's descending allowed Him to take the place of captivity, and the one who was holding people there, and lead them captive - or in other words, capture them.

He did all this to *give gifts unto men* - or literally, to give *the gift* unto *all people*. This is important. What is *the gift?* The gift the Father has bestowed through His son is summed up in our adoption as sons, and encompasses the gift of salvation, redemption, sanctification, justification and righteousness.

So where Adam fell, Christ has descended in order to lead out the captive maker. So, both his ability to make captives and the very place he uses for captivity now belong to the Son! Look at what John has to say:

Revelation 1:18 - *I [am] He who lives, and was dead, and behold, I am alive forevermore. Amen. And I have the keys of Hades and of Death.*

The I AM is alive forevermore, and holds the keys of the place of captivity and him that leads people into captivity. Therefore, there is now nothing left to hold us down,

215

nothing left to cause us to descend. The Son has descended in our fallen place; He has stepped down into our darkness as one of us. But He did not stay there; neither did He leave us there. He has ascended, also.

> **Psalm 68:18** - *You have ascended on high, You have led captivity captive; You have received gifts among men, Even [from] the rebellious, That the LORD God might dwell [there].*

Hundreds of years before Christ's sacrifice, we have a prophetic word given. Notice how closely it mirrors Paul's words in Ephesians, save one point. Where Paul points out that Jesus Christ has *given* gifts to people, David says He has *received gifts among men (people).* Literally, this says something so powerful. David says *He has received the gift of Adam, even the rebellious.* Jesus Christ has ascended, taken fallen man from his fallen state, even the rebellious ones, and seated us at the right hand of the Father. This truth cannot be overlooked nor thrown to the side. If we are seated at His right hand with the Son as sons ourselves, we have some inalienable rights.

> **Galatians 3:29** - *And if you [are] Christ's, then you are Abraham's seed, and heirs according to the promise.*

What a powerful verse this is when we fully understand the process of adoption by the Father through

Christ. This little word *heirs* means *one who receives his allotted possession by right of sonship*, not someone who was simply added to the last will and testament, but someone who receives by the *right* of sonship. The right of sonship says this: no matter how many attorneys want to come at us, no amount of legalism can ever take away our right to our inheritance. And what is this inheritance? It is the promise of blessing, the promised land - a place of provision and health! This is not some far off, future tense promise; it is a right now, in this place promise!

> **Ephesians 1:4-5** - *just as He chose us in Him before the foundation of the world, that we should be holy and without blame before Him in love, having predestined us to adoption as sons by Jesus Christ to Himself, according to the good pleasure of His will.*

Through the fall of man, there is the descending of Christ. Through the ascension of Christ, there is the ascending of man, as sons of God. We are adopted in love, being holy and blameless, giving pleasure to the Father of all.

CALEB MILLER

CHAPTER 17
ANGELS

"Now this, "He ascended"--what does it mean but that He also first descended into the lower parts of the earth?"
Ephesians 4:9

W E HAVE DISCUSSED much in this revelation that Jesus has not only redeemed humanity, but also, accomplished a complete and utter reversal of all things which were laid bare in the fall. As the one who was with the Father in the beginning, He was alongside the Father breathing life into man, instilling into man a part of His own being. One of the most important things we can understand about Adam is the fact that all people were in Him, both in seed form as the father of all people, and in spiritual form in the fall.

> **Romans 5:18** - *Therefore, as through one man's offense [judgment came] to all men, resulting in condemnation, even so through one Man's righteous act [the free gift came] to all men, resulting in justification of life.*

Many consider that Adam had the unique ability to represent all of humanity in himself. Through his fall, all fell. As a side note, please know Paul says earlier in Romans 5:12 that *Just as through one man sin entered the world ... and spread to all men ...* then leads to verse 18, the free gift came to all people resulting in justification of life to all people. How did the fall come to all people? Was it by their choosing, their belief or their confession? Was it by their faith, their repentance or their devotion to Adam? No! The fall came to all, regardless of whether or not they wanted it, chose it, believed in it or accepted it. *Just as* means *in the same way as,* or *even as.* So even as the fall came, justification came. This is hard for us to swallow, but Paul clearly outlined it for us. He let us know that without our choosing, Christ completely justified us in life. And what is more, He brought the free gift to all people. Now again, religion tries to tell us that a gift is only ours if we receive it; however, this is not what Paul is saying. The free gift results in justification of life. Jesus took care of not only delivering the gift to humanity, but He also *opened* it, which is the very reason Paul uses the past tense here, *came to all men.*

Back to Adam: Adam did have the ability to bind all people in himself in the fall; however, this ability was not unique. Adam could only possess that which he had inherited from the Father's Son during the moment of creation. Adam is known as a type and shadow of Christ. He is the image of Jesus, and as such, can only possess that which the Son has already possessed and has given him. The ability to bind all people in himself came directly from Christ, and as a sort of cosmic leapfrog, came back to Christ through the lineage of Adam. We must get this. The gospel's very nature is that all people were bound in Christ apart from their choosing. Who among us was alive to choose to be in Him when He died? (The Apostle Paul says if one died for all then all have died). Because of this, Adam also had the ability to hopelessly bind all people in himself.

This is why this principle of the divine reversal is so important; and, I consider it foundational to our understanding of scriptural principles. Until we are able to grasp that just as the first Adam bound all of humanity in himself, in the same fashion, the last Adam bound all of humanity in Himself, we will fail to see the power, beauty and inclusion of the gospel. We will cling to *Christianese* like free will and choice. Often times what we are really referring to is autonomy. We are not robots, simply being played by a great white bearded puppet master in the sky. We are unique beings with divine traces all over our DNA. Do we have the power of choice? Of course we do, but our choice will never supersede His. Now, we need to proceed to a powerful truth in this principle of the divine reversal of all things. To do so, we will go back to Genesis and discover what happened just after the fall.

Gen 3:22-24 – *Then the LORD God said, "Behold, the man has become like one of Us, to know good and evil. And now, lest he put out his hand and take also of the tree of life, and eat, and live forever"–therefore the LORD God sent him out of the garden of Eden to till the ground from which he was taken. So He drove out the man; and He placed cherubim at the east of the garden of Eden, and a flaming sword which turned every way, to guard the way to the tree of life.*

First of all, we need to take note that God says *man has become like one of Us*. If we do not believe in the Trinitarian nature of the Godhead, then who is God talking to? Secondly, the intent has always been that only the Godhead should know good and evil. We were never meant to know this. We were only ever meant to know our Father, with no judgment of good or evil.

If we continue on, we will see that the Father did not simply run man out of the garden and talk to him from the gate. No, the Father came out with man to signify His willingness to endure humanity's sin and be intimately involved with the supposed tarnish that clouded humanity's vision.

What we will focus on is this cherubim (angel) God put at the gate of the garden. This is a guardian angel that the Father placed there; not to keep man from tending the garden or eating the approved plants, but to keep him from eating the tree of life. This angel was to protect the way to life and guard the garden so no other person could eat of the tree of life, not just Adam or Eve. We must understand that there is nothing more devastating than separation plus eternal life, living eternally separated from the Father, which is exactly what the Father was trying to protect mankind from!

Then, man began a sacrificial system to appease what they believed was the desire of the Father. They saw the warning, *the day you eat of it, dying you will die,* as the apparent blood lust of the Father, and their desire was to appease the blood lust, and in some fashion to stave off their own death. Still today, we maintain that the Father wanted the sacrificial system in order to offer us redemption. However, David says in Psalm 40:6 – *sacrifice and offering you did not desire,* and, this is echoed by the author in Hebrews 10:5 and 8 – *sacrifice and offering you did not desire.* This is a large topic, but we need to grasp it. The Father did not desire sacrifice! Man thought He wanted death; so, man offered death. Ever willing to work within our framework of understanding, the Father decided to work all things for our good, and used our own sacrificial systems to offer us a temporary redemption of sins. God, who knows all things from the beginning, saw this system in place, and the Son decided to join in the Father's knowledge and He made the plan to use our own system to trap us. When the Father spoke *the day you eat of it, dying you will die,* He was not referring to a literal day, or even the mortal life of Adam and Eve. The Hebrew word for *day* is *yown,* and can mean a day, or a period, or an age. The Father was telling Adam, *because my Son has bound all men in Him, you have as well, and in the day – the age – that you eat of this, you will necessitate the sacrifice of the Son, who, in binding all people in himself, will bring death to all.* This is a paradigm shift, I know, but a greatly necessary one! The Father is prophesying our vicarious suicide. Since we had the idea about the Father wanting blood, the systems we created became the very systems He used to bring His word to pass. In His eyes, dying is a blessing not a curse! We all died with Christ; so we all might be raised and seated with Him!

The same cherubim used to guard the way to the garden, the Father orders to be placed on the Ark of the Covenant, with their wings spread, covering the mercy seat. Mercy seat is *kapporeth* and literally means *the place of atonement.* What is atonement? There are several meanings, but the most literal translation is *to make reconciliation.* Man views atonement as something else receiving punishment in their stead; but, the Father has a bit of a different view of atonement. These cherubim are placed over the seat of reconciliation where the Father's will is accomplished. His desire has always been for mankind's reconciliation. This is why *God was in Christ reconciling the world unto Himself, not imputing their trespasses against them;* and, the reason we were given the same ministry of reconciliation. His heart's desire was to see all people reconciled to Himself; therefore, He accomplished it through the Son.

Now we fast forward now to the moment when humanity was forever rendered alive, at the resurrection of

Christ. John beautifully lays this occurrence out for us in his gospel.

John 20:12 - *And she saw two angels in white sitting, one at the head and the other at the feet, where the body of Jesus had lain.*

Mary came back to the tomb where Jesus was and looked inside of it. She saw the bed where His body was laid. What she saw on the bed were two angels - one at the head and the other at the foot. Now, the picture begins to stack up nicely, does it not? We have this vision of the place of reconciliation in the Old Testament surrounded on either end by two cherubim, or guardian angels. However, these angels in Jesus' tomb were not guardian angels but *aggelos* - messenger angels, declarers!

Interestingly, Matthew records one angel, outside the tomb; Mark reports "a man" inside the tomb; Luke writes about two "men" in the tomb; and John says these two angels sat. In all cases, the angels say things like "do not be afraid". The message of the gospel is this: *Do not be afraid.* From the birth of John the Baptist, to the birth of Jesus Christ, to the ministry of Christ, to His resurrection, and on to His appearance to the disciples, the message has always been *do not be afraid.* Even the eternal Christ in the book of Revelation greets John with *do not be afraid.* Why is this? *Because fear involves torment* (1 John 1:18). Only love can cast out fear, and only the one whose DNA is love can have the authority to say *fear not.* Moving on.

In the Old Testament protecting angels guarded the seat of the reconciliation of humanity. However, in the New Testament, proclaimers now surrounded the seat of the finalization of humanity's reconciliation! They were placed there to announce the finalization of humanity's reconciliation.

But wait, there is more!

Ephesians 4:8-10 - *Therefore He says: "When He ascended on high, He led captivity captive, And gave gifts to men." (Now this, "He ascended"-- what does it mean but that He also first descended into the lower parts of the earth? He who descended is also the One who ascended far above all the heavens, that He might fill all things.)*

Because the gospel writers did not know what was going on while Jesus lay in the grave, Paul says something for us, which is not outlined in the gospels. Remember, Paul spent time alone with Christ Himself, who told him the message of grace, and made him privy to what happened while Jesus was in the grave. Paul says *he descended into the lower parts of the earth* to let us know that during Christ's time of sleep, He entered into our hell and *led captivity captive*. Remember, the word *captivity* in the Greek means both the place of captivity and the one who holds people there. This says that Christ took the captives, the place of captivity, and the one who holds them there and led them out. His work brought all to a place of resurrected, new life.

We should revisit Genesis quickly. *He placed cherubim at the east of the Garden of Eden, and a flaming sword which turned every way, to guard the way to the tree of life.* The Father placed this guardian angel at the entrance to guard the way to life. In the tomb of Christ we not only see two angels placed to declare the completion of mankind's reconciliation, but also, we see angels set in place at the tomb's entrance to guard the way back to a place where Christ had been. That place was death!

Why there were different accounts given for the four different gospels, I do not know. I believe the people saw what they needed to see. Some needed a flaming sword in the form of a bright light to remind them the way was closed.

Christ has so utterly and completely reversed the fall; and yet we continue to live today as though Adam were more successful in his fall than Christ was in His ascension. We do not have a failure for a savior, but an ultimate and complete success! Adam could only do what was inside him from the Son. In binding all people in himself, he forever sealed their fate in Christ.

THE DIVINE REVERSAL

- Where Christ breathed into man, He had the authority to breathe their last on the cross.
- Where Adam dispersed humanity, Christ has consummated all people in Himself.
- Where Adam brought shame, disgrace, dishonor, and discredit, Christ has relieved us.
- Where Adam brought exile, Christ brought inclusion.
- Where Adam fell, and bound all, Christ ascended, binding the same *all* that were bound in the fall.
- Where Adam lost his own humanity, Christ stepped into humanity and offered us all He is, including His own divine nature.
- Where Adam had his side opened to bring forth a bride, then closed up, Christ had his side opened and left the way so the bride could forever enter in.
- Where the angels over the Ark of the Covenant guarded the seat of reconciliation, the angels in the tomb of Christ proclaim the finishing of humanity's reconciliation.
- Where the angel in the garden blocked the way to life, the angels in the tomb guard the way to death.

I believe there are no small coincidences in the word. I firmly believe the Father does all things for our good, even at the expense of Himself and how humanity may perceive Him. He has accomplished so much through the power of His Son, and to try to sum those accomplishments up in one book, one teaching, one song, or one statement is an endeavor destined to fail. My hope is that we have at least covered enough to give you a bigger vision of Jesus Christ, His fulfillment of all things, and His utter and complete reversal of the fall of man.

SOME THOUGHTS ON "DESTINATIONAL CHRISTIANITY"

HEAVEN OR HELL? This book was nearly begun with this chapter, and it might seem odd to start a book about the nature of grace or the effectual work of the cross with a statement like this. However, this is what the Christian church has done to the world. This type of approach has affected our evangelism, the books we write, and the series we teach. It has even caused a dividing line among the body of Christ on whether or not we believe in the existence of a literal hell, a figurative one, or a hell reserved only for the devil and his angels. It is not our belief in hell that saves us, provides for us, or made the way for us to approach our Father. Yet, it has become more important than the One who *did* accomplish all these things, Jesus Christ. We care less about the person of Christ and His love for mankind than we do about whether or not someone believes in, or teaches, hell. We want to know the end result, and the final goal. We are not so concerned with how we get there, but we should be.

The truth is that the journey is actually far more important than the destination. What if I were to tell you I bought you a dinner for two in Hawaii? That might bless you a little; but what would probably be better is for me to tell you I have actually purchased two airline tickets for you and a friend to go to Hawaii. Your ticket has been purchased. The Father handed the whole world the ticket of His Son; and we spend our lives talking about the destination. We *evangelize* by asking strangers if they know where they will go after they die. Does this sound like the Father? Does it sound like what the Son would say? Does it sound like what Jesus said while He walked this earth? Of course, the answers are NO! You see, Jesus did one thing far greater than just talking of destinations; He restored identity.

This "destinational" type of Christianity is a bit of a plague in our lives today. We tell the world they will go to hell if they do not believe in Jesus. We pound our pulpits loudly proclaiming their sin and folly; we forsake love, all in an attempt to *win* people to Christ.

Jesus Christ has already won. He has taken the keys of death and hell (Rev. 1:18); and He holds those keys, not as a bully holds our lunch money just out of reach, but as a loving, caring Savior. He has forever hidden those keys in His very person, safely tucked away from the hands of man and something even greater, He is not dangling them over us, just waiting to drop the hammer - so to speak.

I want to look at something:

> **Matthew 6:34** - *Therefore do not worry about tomorrow, for tomorrow will worry about its own things. Sufficient for the day [is] its own trouble.*

The KJV renders this verse *take therefore no thought*. Notice Jesus says *no thought*, not *a little thought, some thought, lots of thought*, or *every thought*. He is laying something out for us; and we often miss it. He is saying *do not worry about your future, your eternity, or even your destination.*

What do we do though? We base our entire Christian existence on the so-called truth that our calling is to tell people about heaven and hell. Nothing could be farther from the truth. Our calling is not to warn people of their final destination, or (and this might touch your religion a little bit) to rejoice in our final destination. Our call is to live our lives today to the fullest possible. Jesus said in John 10:10 He came so we should have life (*zoe* life - literally animation) and have it abundantly (*perissos* - literally, more than is needed, superior and uncommon). This kind of highly animated, more-than-is-needed life is something that

233

pertains to our physical lives. Salvation is just that, a super-human physical existence.

Jesus has told us to take no thought for tomorrow, and then said that He came to give us abundant life. That alone should be enough for us to weigh our current theology, doctrinal discourses, and approach to evangelism. However, let us look quickly at what John the Baptist had to say.

Luke 3:5-6 - *Every valley shall be filled And every mountain and hill brought low; The crooked places shall be made straight And the rough ways smooth; And all flesh shall see the salvation of God.*

Jesus came to give us not only abundant life; He came to fill every valley, bring down every mountain and hill, straighten every crooked place, and smooth out all the rough patches.

Where I live there are mountains, plains, rivers, valleys, and rocky areas. This verse says much to me. For me to go into our mountains and view a natural version of what John was saying is staggering. John was proclaiming one thing, which is this: the way Jesus is preparing is so easy and so simple to navigate that the only natural conclusion in John's mind was simply all flesh would see the salvation of God.

My father best summed up what I am trying to express. In one of his messages, he simply said "600" and then went on to say, "now figure out how to get there". This is what we do in our own lives. Our "600" is heaven or hell.

We start there and then, we begin working backwards on how to get there, or avoid there, depending on which place we are discussing. Inevitably, the problem with this approach is that there are those who will decide 100 x 6 is the way to 600; then, there will be others who will decide that 6 + 6 (100 times) is the way to 600 and, still others will decide that 240 x 2.5 is the way.

What is the problem with all of this? They are all correct; however, what they are saying is that their way of reaching 600 is the *right* way. When we start with an eternal, final issue, we have nowhere to go. However, if we will start with what Jesus Christ has done, and what that means for you and me, then the eternal destination will take care of itself!

I would like to invite you to erase your chalkboard, calculator, iPhone, or paper in order to take off the final destination. From the beginning, look with me at the Father, His perfect Son, The Holy Spirit and the communion they share, which we have been offered freely, and have been invited to share with them. If we can do this together, denominational lines can be crossed, doctrinal dogma redefined, and the world will begin to hear a resounding call from the heart of the Father - "You Are Included!"

PAUL AND HELL

The man the majority considers the foremost authority on the word of the Father's grace would have to be the Apostle Paul. Paul taught more firmly on the word of grace than anyone else. He taught more deeply on the love of the Father, and, he taught more often on the finished work of Christ. He wrote letters to all of Asia, Rome, Greece, and Judea. He was an Apostle, Pastor, Teacher, Missionary, and Theologian. He spent time alone in the desert being ministered to by the very One Who had done the work, and received the message he would spend the rest of his life teaching.

Paul taught about evangelism, spoke on sexual morality and conduct, wrote to pastors about living Godly lives and spoke to marriage partners about love and submission. He wrote to men about how to be Godly men, to women about being Godly women, to children about obedience, to elders, teachers, pastors, leaders, deacons, and all other sorts of church inner-ministerial jobs. He wrote to Jew and Gentile, regarding none above the other. It would seem to me that Paul's ministry was something of an all-encompassing teaching and preaching ministry.

Yet, there is one subject Paul seemed to leave out of the majority of his writings, in any format, and that was the subject of *Hell*.

What does this say to me? Well, it does not tell me hell is not real, that Paul didn't believe in hell, or that nobody is going there. It tells me much like we have just been discussing, that Paul had a revelation that did not need to include fear of judgment, fear of punishment, or fear of retribution. His revelation was Christ crucified, the never-ending grace of the Father, and the love of God for all mankind. We could take a good dose of Paul's teaching today and use it in our own lives, our churches, our home groups, and our relationships, and never even worry about discussing hell.

We are told that perfect love casts out all fear; so then, why would we want to use fear to try to introduce people to the one who *is* love? The Father exists in and consists of love. It is who He is and what He gives. There is no place for fear in love. After we have already come to know and believe the love the Father has for us, we need to leave this discussion to an afterthought.

If we preach Christ, the identity of man *in* Christ, and the risen and powerful savior of the world, hell pales in comparison. Why would I want to discuss a place of eternal damnation and suffering, when I can discuss a person whose beauty is unmatched, whose sacrifice is complete, and whose love is unchallenged? I would not. So I will not.

The point of all this is simple: we need to focus together on what is important in our lives, which is the risen Jesus Christ, the fact that He has included all of humanity in His finished work, and that we now have reconciliation with the Father.

CALEB MILLER

CONCLUSION

I firmly believe that Paul instructed us to teach one thing, Jesus Christ and Him crucified. When we preach Christ, we preach victory, victory over sin, victory over death, victory over hell, victory over satan, victory over sickness, and victory over every problem we could ever face. However, when we preach sin, death, hell, satan, sickness or our problems, we have done something which we probably never intended. We have used the very breath of life that resides in us to breathe life back into something that was rendered dead at the cross of Christ.

My call, as is the call of every minister, evangelist, preacher or Christian for that matter, is to minister reconciliation. Not just any reconciliation, but the reconciliation that says, "God was in Christ, reconciling the world unto Himself". The Father has taken such great care in ushering us into adoption, into His very family, that we do Him a great disservice and His gospel a terrible injustice by preaching anything but this reconciliation. If we leave our arguments behind and forge forward with the revelation of the love of the Father, the very revelation with which Jesus left us, we will see all manner of things happen. One of those is the answer to the question of eternity.

If we want people to believe, then we need to stop trying to convince them of the historical Jesus or whether or not He spoke of a literal hell, a figurative one, or something completely different, and begin revealing the ever-loving, peace-making, all-forgiving, judgment-taking, water-into-wine-turning, always-healing, crucified, dead, buried, resurrected, successful, wonderful, fear-not-speaking Savior of the world!

ABOUT THE AUTHOR

I am a recording artist, a teacher, an author, a worship leader, and a pastor. As a recording artist, I have written dozens of songs all from the standpoint of the Father's love for His children. As a teacher I strive to teach this same truth, that God so loved the WORLD… As an author, my hope is always to convey this truth in a way that has the ability to reach into the lives of the reader. As a pastor, I hope to always minister the power of the Father's love to everyone I come into contact with.

Beyond (or rather above) all that though, I am a committed father and husband. Having children has a unique way of changing one's view of the Father, and I am no exception. Through my children, the Father has often spoken to me about His love for His own children, using them as examples of grace and love. I often say that having kids will ruin your theology, and mine are no exception. Being a husband has the powerful ability to show a man just how deeply the Father wants to care for him in all his endeavors. While I do not necessarily view myself as a "bride" of Christ in the typical religious sense, the marriage metaphor serves as a wonderful reminder of our union with the Godhead, His protection of us, and His provision for all of His family.

Caleb is currently serving in a pastoral role at The Father's House, a church in Northern Colorado (US) with the vision of revealing Jesus in, to, and with you at all times. The primary goal of the ministry is to create a place where people burned who are out on religion, tired of performing, and seeking a place of rest can gather and feel at home.

He can be reached through the ministry website at www.fathershousefc.com.